The Art of Professional Communication

Going beyond the mechanics of professional communication, this book combines insights into the overlooked implicit demands of corporate communication challenges with the proven strategies and techniques that distinguish professionals as capable communicators and candidates for promotion.

The practical strategies offered in this book represent professional communication principles filtered through the lens of the author's 40-year career, that enabled him to rise from an initial assignment as a technical editor to positions of senior management directing large, diverse business and technical organizations. Here, he has collected into one resource the reasoned and disciplined decision-making processes, tools, and techniques essential to craft communications, precisely attuned to the explicit and implicit expectations of each assignment and supported by a structure and presentation logic that delivers a totally responsive and accurately targeted product. This is an essential guide for all levels of professionals who recognize the need to distinguish themselves within a highly competitive career environment.

Business professionals and instructors in corporate training programs, supervisors and managers, and students in professional communication programs will welcome this deep dive into the real-world challenges and opportunities in professional communication and the role effective communication plays in career advancement.

Dr. Daniel L. Plung is a recognized leader in professional communication. In addition to chairing and keynoting professional communication conferences, he has more than 50 publications, including two college textbooks. His teaching experience at three major US universities is complemented by a 45-year career providing leadership on multibillion-dollar projects in both the US and the UK, encompassing responsibility for all phases from proposal development to contract closeout.

The Art of Professional Communication

Strategies that Advance Careers

Daniel L. Plung

Routledge
Taylor & Francis Group

NEW YORK AND LONDON

Designed cover image: Getty

First published 2025
by Routledge
605 Third Avenue, New York, NY 10158

and by Routledge
4 Park Square, Milton Park, Abingdon, Oxon, OX14 4RN

Routledge is an imprint of the Taylor & Francis Group, an informa business

Library of Congress Cataloguing-in-Publication Data
Names: Plung, Daniel L., author.
Title: The art of professional communication : strategies that advance careers / Daniel L. Plung.
Description: New York, NY : Routledge, 2024. | Includes bibliographical references and index. |
Identifiers: LCCN 2024015724 (print) | LCCN 2024015725 (ebook) | ISBN 9781032596501 (hardback) | ISBN 9781032596488 (paperback) | ISBN 9781003455585 (ebook)
Subjects: LCSH: Communication in management. | Communication in organizations. | Business communication.
Classification: LCC HD30.3 .P58 2024 (print) | LCC HD30.3 (ebook) | DDC 658.4/5--dc23/eng/20240404
LC record available at https://lccn.loc.gov/2024015724
LC ebook record available at https://lccn.loc.gov/2024015725

ISBN: 978-1-032-59650-1 (hbk)
ISBN: 978-1-032-59648-8 (pbk)
ISBN: 978-1-003-45558-5 (ebk)

DOI: 10.4324/9781003455585

Typeset in Sabon
by MPS Limited, Dehradun

To my family that continuously inspires me; to the professional colleagues who have given my career meaning and purpose; and to the hundreds of students who have taught me more than I could ever teach them, I offer this book as a modest "thank you."

Contents

Preface

Understanding and mastering the communication skills that go beyond the basics and get professionals noticed require study and practice. They are skills that must be complemented by disciplined communication strategies.

The melding of a 40+ year career in leadership assignments with an academic background teaching professional communication in college classrooms and corporate training centers has allowed me to isolate these unique strategies and communication techniques. And, equally important, years of mentoring professionals have taught me the means to make those lessons meaningful, interesting, and memorable.

Placing that history in context, this text is intended as if my "last lecture series"—the compilation and summation of critical lessons forged over time and proven by the professional successes of numerous students who have learned and diligently applied them.

Examining a principal component of a robust business communication capability, each chapter begins with a short vignette illustrating the lesson's themes and providing both a practical context for the instruction and a proven memory aid. Highlighting communication factors as diverse as those that cost General Motors hundreds of millions of dollars to those that contributed to Florence Nightingale's groundbreaking visualization of the human cost of the Crimean War ensures the essence of each lesson will be long retained.

Illustrating the strategies that distinguish exceptional communicators, this book lays out *The Art of Professional Communication* and provides you with *Strategies that Advance Careers*.

Introduction

The Promotable Executive

Professional communication and business communication texts, as well as the popular literature, cite communication as an essential attribute expected of professionals and as a critical antecedent to getting ahead in industry. Responding to this need to train effective communicators, current textbooks place an emphasis on facility with conciseness in writing, audience, and document formatting protocols.

Although these areas of attention are clearly important, they are not broad enough to cover the actual communication challenges professionals experience, and clearly are not sufficient to distinguish individuals as capable communicators, nor to distinguish them as professionals warranting consideration for promotion.

To achieve a level of skill at which one is recognized as an accomplished communicator, particularly as one climbs the corporate ladder, professionals must be completely prepared to deal with the complexity, urgency, and significance of assignments that routinely arise in the management and leadership of business and industry. Professionals must be prepared to provide responses that are complete, well-structured, well-argued, clearly presented, and specifically responsive to the affected audiences.

To that point, we begin here by exploring an actual case in which a set of communication failures cost a major corporation its reputation and billions of dollars. Using perspective gained from consideration of that case, we will explore the evolution of contemporary professional and business communication instruction to explain its current orientation and, thereby, lay the groundwork for more fully appreciating the types of challenges professionals encounter and the tools, techniques, and strategies needed to meet them.

Anatomy of a Communication Catastrophe

Over a 14-year period beginning with the initial recognition of the problem in 2001, General Motors (GM) struggled with what might have seemed to be a straightforward engineering problem. The ignition

DOI: 10.4324/9781003455585-1

switch installed in numerous makes and models had been designed to turn effortlessly, ostensibly simulating the feel of an expensive European sports car; however, when jostled (by a bumpy stretch of road or the driver's knee hitting the keys), the switch tended to turn from the "run" to the "accessory" position.

In that position, the switch turned off the engine—stalling the car and disabling the power steering, anti-lock brakes, and airbags. In engineering terms, the "torque" was not right on the switch. In human terms, drivers were being killed and injured. By the time GM acknowledged the problem, 124 people had been killed and 3,000 injured. Emerging from beneath the avalanche of investigations and settlements, GM's failures to act judiciously cost the company approximately $2.6 billion.

Although GM's multi-year challenge was principally attending to redefining the anatomy of the ignition switch, untangling the mystery of the vehicle's complex wiring, and realigning system interfaces, another element of GM's "incompetence"—as Congressman Murphy of Pennsylvania labeled it during the Senate investigation—was becoming apparent. As *Fortune* magazine accurately noted in light of several Congressional investigations, GM's actions and decision-making had failed owing to a "catastrophic breakdown in communications."[1]

That "breakdown" began on November 19, 2004, when an internal GM executive committee met to review reports of vehicles being "keyed off." Using a four-point severity scale, with 1 being significant safety issues and 4 being "annoyances," GM's Production Improvement Team assigned the malfunctioning switches a rating of 3, classifying the problem as a "customer convenience," not a consequential safety problem. That mislabeling of the problem was in large measure a consequence of one of three pervasive communication issues that, for almost a decade, precluded GM from understanding the technical problem and from taking prudent action: (1) cabining information; (2) evasive and misleading language; and (3) unclear presentation of information.

"Cabining" of Information

The principal reason for initially mislabeling the ignition switch problem was that only one member of the review team—comprised of a cross-section of engineers and business personnel—understood that losing engine power would preclude deployment of the airbags. Although the information should have been known to all members of the executive committee, GM had a culture that restricted the flow of information among organizations and between management and company leadership.

As summed up by the CEO in advance of Congressional hearings: "Repeatedly, individuals failed to disclose critical pieces of information that could have fundamentally changed the lives of those impacted by a faulty ignition switch."[2] This fracturing—or cabining—of information not only limited effectiveness of decision-making, it also eliminated personal accountability:

> *The ... Ignition Switch issue passed through an astonishing number of committees ... [Committees] flagged the issue, proposed a solution, and the solution died in a committee or with some other ad hoc group exploring the issue. This practice of promoting inaction made determining the identity of any actual decision-maker ... impenetrable. No single person owned any decision.*[3]

Well ingrained in the GM culture, this avoidance of accountability was referred to as the "GM salute": "a crossing of the arms and pointing outward towards others, indicating that the responsibility belongs to someone else, not me."[4]

Evasive and Misleading Language

As early as 2005, GM began minimizing public knowledge of the magnitude of the switch problem. Approached by the media that year, the GM safety manager shrugged off the "inconvenience," suggesting the issue was relatively insignificant since cars remained "drivable."[5] When pressure mounted later that same year, GM issued a vaguely worded Technical Service Bulletin (TSB) to car dealers, noting a "potential for the driver to inadvertently turn off the ignition due to the low ignition key cylinder torque."[6] No mention of "stalling" was made "precisely because GM believed customers might associate stalling with a safety problem."[7] Customers were simply advised to remove heavy items from key rings.

Promoting evasive language, employees were warned to write "smart." Making direct statements (e.g., "Dangerous ... almost caused accident") was to be avoided, as were "hot" terms. Words such as "problem," "safety," and "defect" were to be replaced, respectively, by "issue," "potential safety implication," and "does not perform to design." Moreover, concerned such direction might become public knowledge, employees "did not take notes at all at critical safety meetings because they believed GM lawyers did not want such notes taken."[8]

Unclear Presentation of Information

When opportunities did occur to inform senior management or the GM Board of Directors, the mandated lack of candor translated into incomprehensible and unactionable presentations. As example, one presentation to an executive committee offered this veiled and circular explanation of how failures occurred:

> *If a crash event has started while in power mode RUN, any transition from power mode to RUN is ignored until the crash event is completed—and the power mode is recorded as RUN in EDR [the vehicle's event data recorder].*[9]

At the same time, when information was prepared for presentation to the Board of Directors regarding ignition switches, it was only included as one of 52 "backup" slides (slides generally shown only if a related question is asked by a Board member). Never shown, the slide, in keeping with the established culture, made no reference to the mounting numbers of injuries, deaths, or the financial implications of switches keying off.

In the end, perhaps most appalling is that had GM taken a more prudent, professional, and ethical response to its problems, the total estimated cost it would have incurred was on the order of $26 million—$10 per each of the 2.6 million affected vehicles! Acting prudently would have retained the company's reputation; it also would have saved the careers of 15 senior professionals and GM executives who were terminated from an array of departments—engineering, legal, quality assurance, public policy, and human resources—clearly highlighting the pervasiveness of the communication issues.

Broadly stated, the GM saga identifies several important expectations of senior professionals: (1) acting ethically; (2) assuming personal accountability; (3) delivering thorough, accurate, and readily understood communications; and (4) promoting the effective and shared use of information to advance the mission and values of the company—all essential facets of one's professional communcation responsibilities.

Yet, the GM saga also raises an important question: Why would a community of highly educated professionals consciously or willingly participate in such a "catastrophic breakdown in communications"?

The Disconnect between Instruction and Practice

Consistent with the commonly voiced assertion that "communication" is important and among the most valued skills in business and industry, subscribers to the *Harvard Business Review* rated the "ability to communicate" as the most important "characteristic of a promotable executive," ranking the skills higher than ambition, education, or capacity for hard work.[10] Supporting this contention, a survey examining 1,000 advertisements for full-time positions in marketing, general management, finance, and human resources management reported that "communication" was not only the most commonly cited desired skill overall; with the exception of skills specific to the disciplines reviewed, it was also the most highly cited desired skill in each of the four professions studied.[11]

Yet, despite this widespread interest in hiring professionals with "an ability to communicate," there is no commonly shared definition of what such skills should entail. Rather, it is probable companies assume appropriate skills are obtained through the standard courses in business and professional communication. That instruction, as evaluated in a review of numerous communication textbooks, indicated the majority of instruction pertains to communication models (e.g., writing business letters), making presentations, and writing and speaking concisely.[12]

Although needed, it is obvious these skills bear little correspondence to promoting the capabilities or behaviors that would have mitigated the communication problems evidenced at GM. However, although acknowledging this gap between instruction and practice is a first step, in order to arrive at a more functional and practical set of lessons and communication strategies, we should understand how this curriculum was established.

Derivation of the Disconnect

Although backing all the way up to the writings of Aristotle, Cicero, and Quintilian can provide context to this inquiry, the more immediate underpinnings of our contemporary instruction derive from developments in the 19th century. Early in that century, driven by mounting attention to the sciences and technology, expanding public education, and growing reliance on the popular vernacular rather than Latin, universities shifted instructional emphasis from speech to writing—profoundly announced by elocution and composition courses displacing traditional rhetoric.

During this period, a wealth of philosophers and rhetoricians sought to weigh in on how best to navigate this shift in educational emphasis. To simplify and abbreviate the explanation, we can most directly trace that evolution by considering three of the most influential voices who, spanning the length of the 19th century, were central to defining what were to become the keystones of contemporary instruction: Hugh Blair, Alexander Bains, and Adam Sherman Hill.

In the early days of the 19th century, Hugh Blair's *Lectures on Rhetoric and Belles Lettres* became the centerpiece of much of the writing instruction in both England and the United States. Concerned with conciseness and the "exact import of precision," Blair contended writers must practice "pruning the expression, so as to exhibit neither more nor less than an exact copy of (the writer's] idea who uses it." Poor writing, he concluded, reflected one of three failings: Not expressing "that idea which the author intends"; expressing an "idea but not quite fully and completely"; or expressing the idea "together with something more than he intends."[13]

This line of reasoning was subsequently picked up in mid-19th century by Alexander Bain's *English Composition and Rhetoric: A Manual*. With its stated goal to "methodize instruction in English Composition," theory was transitioned into practicable classroom instruction. Precision (or "economy" as Bain referred to it) was a physiological imperative driving selection of words and the formulation of sentences and paragraphs: "Every word uttered taxes the attention and occupies a space in the thoughts; hence when words are used only as instruments, they should be compressed into the least compass consistent with the adequate expression of the meaning."[14]

Extending this concept of "adequate expression," Bain's methodizing advocated emulating the structure of established communication models. As he proposed, rather than the Aristotelian tradition which categorized speeches in terms of their purpose (pursuing justice, offering praise, or attempts at persuasion), to Bain writing effectively meant practicing five "kinds of composition": Description, Narration, Exposition, Oratory, and Poetry.

With this alignment of precision and communication models as the fundamentals of instruction, there remained only one more factor to complete the foundations of contemporary professional communication studies.

That last factor—providing a practical orientation for the instruction—was introduced by Herbert Spencer, a world-renowned scientist and political theorist (perhaps best remembered for coining the phrase "survival of the fittest"). In *Philosophy of Style,* directed at his scientific colleagues, Spencer asserted that "The more time and attention it takes to receive and understand each sentence, the less time and attention can be given to the contained idea; and the less vividly will that idea be conceived."[15] That argument, in keeping with Bain's approach, was soon "methodized."

In *The Principles of Rhetoric and Their Application,* Adam Sherman Hill began by further displacing the Aristotelian tradition of rhetoric: He proclaimed rhetoric was no longer a function of logic or reasoning, but rather a reflection of precision. Rhetoric, he declared, "may be defined as the art of efficient communication by language." Having totally freed composition from its original roots, Hill, in a single sentence, sounds the call that ushers in a major change in pedagogy: "Rhetoric should be studied at school and in college, not as a science, but as an art with practical ends in view."[16]

It is not long after publication of Hill's treatise that the "practical ends" of composition combined with the pedagogical concentration on precision and replicating of communication models form what we now accept as the framework for contemporary instruction in business and professional communication.

The Current Divide

Within the first two decades of the new century, the first two composition texts specifically intended for use by students and professionals in business and science were published.

Responding to "the current demand for a brief presentation of the principal rules of good English grammar, sentence structure, paragraphing, punctuation, capitalization, letter writing, and report making adapted to the needs of business," in 1915, George Hotchkiss published his *Handbook of Business English*.[17] A decade later, a companion text is published providing similar "methodizing" for use in the sciences.

"In this modern age of science and industry, we are compelled to think clearly and to speak and write concisely."[18] So begins the preface of Philip McDonald's 1929 book on *English and Science*. Clearly delineating his intended market, McDonald continues by asserting that "much of the old-fashioned rhetoric and composition ... is not suitable for the education of engineers, scientists, and most business and professional people."

Complementing discussions of grammar, punctuation, and conciseness (which he credits as "The Cardinal Secret of Style"), McDonald shifts the emphasis of instruction to the study of communication models. He devotes the majority of his text to detailing the proper structuring and formatting of technical papers, reports, and business letters—forever establishing discipline-specific communication models as the backbone of communication specializations in business, technical, and professional communication.

With this final fusing of brevity, precision, and communication models as the principal substance of instruction targeting industry and the sciences, we now have the complete genealogy of our standard communication curriculum.

The Inherited Legacy

Although modern-day topics such as communication technology, intercultural communication, and group dynamics are often included in today's courses, the instructional core has remained largely unchanged from that laid out in the 19th and early decades of the 20th centuries.

Acknowledging the broad acceptance of this curriculum, a book coincidentally entitled *Who's Going to Run General Motors?* focused expressly on defining "what college students need to learn today to become business leaders of tomorrow." Among the seven fundamental skills needed, communication was number one.

Dramatically characterizing the dimensions of those communication skills that supposedly contribute to success in business, the authors defer to one of their corporate interviewees. The executive's response confirms the acceptance of this narrow educational model: "[Personnel] who aren't skilled at listening simply do not last long. Junior analysts that write 'butchered memos' can forget about promotions. The botched presentation is not soon forgotten."[19]

Although ostensibly acceptable, this limited scope of instruction—as we just learned in the review of GM's situation—can expose a company to poor decision-making, inappropriate responses to challenges, and a less-than-cooperative work environment. And, at the same time, for the professionals who are unprepared for the communication challenges they face, it can mean the difference between corporate advancement and standing idly by as you watch colleagues progress up the corporate ladder.

Positioning to Get Ahead in Business

In attending to the gap between the practical circumstances encountered by professionals and the restricted dimensions of communication instruction, this book presents strategies, techniques, and tools honed over the course of a 40+ year career in industry; taught in college classrooms and corporate training centers; and proven by successful careers of innumerable professionals who have been mentored in these methods.

And the tools and strategies can provide that same boost to your career!

Whether you work at a company the size of GM or at a small business, the lessons are designed to transform a capable communicator into an accomplished communicator, and, in so doing, distinguish individuals with the "characteristics of a promotable executive."

Each chapter represents a step toward getting ahead in business; each strategy is a brick in the foundation that advances careers:

Chapter 1: Knowing What You're Really Supposed to Do—Few assignments (especially as one rises among the ranks of management) are accompanied by a detailed explanation of what is expected or the intended scope. Delivering thorough responses demands careful analysis.

Chapter 2: Making Management's Job Easy—Impressing management requires that you determine who is affected by a challenge, what aspects concern them, and the delivery of tailored, actionable responses.

Chapter 3: Being Quotable—Conciseness and precision alone do not make communications notable. Being noticed, being memorable, requires developing a recognizable personality to your communications.

Chapter 4: Speaking Graphically—Figures, tables, and spreadsheets must be designed to maximize clarity, comprehension, and retention—

artfully balancing communication effectiveness with effective visualization of information.

Chapter 5: Recognizing When Enough Is Enough—Whether in writing, informal conversations, or formal presentations, maintaining a positive reputation means knowing how to self-monitor to ensure you're staying on point and knowing when and how to wrap things up.

Chapter 6: Reasoning Logically—Persuading individuals or teams of a certain conclusion or to take a particular action relies on conveying a convincing argument, and, to the degree appropriate, being prepared to articulate your argument's underlying bases and assumptions.

Chapter 7: Applying Oneself—As a personalized example of how the lessons in this book translate into effective communication, a process is presented for delivering a persuasive application letter, resume, and interview.

Notes

1 Carmen Gallo, "Two Misleading Words Triggered GM's Catastrophic Communication Breakdown," *Forbes*, June 9, 2014, https://www.forbes.com/sites/carminegallo/2014/06/09/two-misleading-words-triggered-gms-catastrophic-communication-breakdown.

2 Gretchen Gavett, "Can GM Make It Safe for Employees to Speak Up?" *Harvard Business Review* 6, June 5, 2014, https://hbr.org/2014/06/can-gm-make-it-safe-for-employees-to-speak-up.

3 Anton Valukas, "Report to Board of Directors of General Motors Company Regarding Ignition Switch Recalls," May 29, 2014, 255, https://www.nhtsa.gov/sites/nhtsa.gov/files/valukas-report-on-gm-redacted.pdf.

4 Valukas, "Report to Board of Directors," 92.

5 Adnan Shaout and Cassandra Desute, "Where Did General Motors Go Wrong with the Ignition Switch Recall?" *IIUM Engineering Journal* 15, no. 2 (2014): 13–21, https://journals.iium.edu.my/ejournal/index.php/iiumej/article/view/522/404.

6 Valukas, p. 92.

7 Valukas, p. 8.

8 Valukas, p. 254.

9 Valukas, p. 173.

10 G.W. Bowman, "What Helps or Harms Promotability?" *Harvard Business Review* 42, no. 6 (January–February 1964): 14.

11 Roger Bennett, "Employers' Demands for Personal Transferable Skills in Graduates: A Content Analysis of 1000 Job Advertisements and an Associated Empirical Study," *Journal of Vocational Education and Training* 54, no. 4 (2002): 457–476.

12 Heather A. Howard, "Communication Practices of Yesteryear: A Qualitative Analysis of Business and Professional Communication Textbooks in the Last Ten Years," Paper Presented at the Annual Meeting of the Speech Communication Society, New Orleans, LA, November 19–22, 1994.

13 Hugh Blair and Abraham Mills, *Lectures on Rhetoric and Belles Letters* (New York: James Conner, 1832), 80, available at https://archive.org/details/lecturesonrheto01millgoog/page/n86/mode/2up?ref=ol&view=theatre.

14 Alexander Bain, *English Composition and Rhetoric: A Manual* (New York: Appleton and Company, 1867), 66.
15 Herbert Spencer, *The Philosophy of Style, an Essay* (New York: Appleton and Company, 1881), 11.
16 Alexander Sherman Hill, *The Principles of Rhetoric and Their Application* (New York: Harper and Brothers, 1897), vii.
17 George Hotchkiss and Edward Kilduff, *Handbook of Business English* (New York: New York University Book Store, 1915), 13.
18 Philip B. McDonald, *English and Science* (New York: D. Van Nostrand Company, Inc., 1929), v.
19 Kenneth Greene and Daniel Seymour, *Who's Going to Run General Motors? What College Students Need to Learn Today to Become the Leaders of Tomorrow* (Princeton, NJ: Peterson's Guides, 1991), 45.

Chapter 1

Knowing What You're Really Supposed to Do

On June 9, 2017, after passengers had been seated on Flight 3411 from Chicago O'Hare International Airport to the Louisville International Airport in Kentucky, the United Airlines staff received a notice: They needed to find seats for two pilots and two flight attendants, who, otherwise, would not be available for their departure assignments in Louisville.

With no empty seats on the plane and no volunteers responding to offers of cash incentives, the airline staff had four passengers removed. "Treating people as an algorithm," as one Senator deemed it in subsequent Congressional hearings, passengers "with the cheapest purchased ticket[s were] booted off."[1]

While three of the four passengers deplaned without incident, the fourth passenger, a 69-year-old doctor, refused to yield his seat. Without considering the reputational, practical, or professional impacts, the crew contacted Airport Security who forcibly removed the doctor. Yanked out of his seat and dragged on his back off the plane, the doctor required hospitalization for injuries including a concussion, broken teeth, and a broken nose.

The day after the incident, United characterized the "the drastic enforcement steps" as an appropriate response to a "stubborn customer." In a memo issued to all United employees, the CEO complimented the crew for "continuing to go above and beyond to ensure we fly right," and stated the passenger's "defiance" had "left [the crew] with no choice."[2]

Attempting to reverse course two weeks later, United, hoping to quell the unrelenting public criticism, issued a *Review and Action Report*. Centered principally on narrow procedural revisions and minor efficiency enhancements, the proposed actions neither addressed the causal factors associated with the Flight 3411 incident nor remedied United's lingering shortcomings. Not surprising given United's performance with Flight 3411, in an industry-wide satisfaction survey, United—in a report section entitled "disenchantment"—was branded as the "industry leader in delays, cancellations, mishandled bags, and bumped passengers."[3]

DOI: 10.4324/9781003455585-2

Although United's proposed remedial actions were misdirected, the forced introspection occasioned by approaching Congressional hearings led both United's CEO and its newly installed President to acknowledge mishandling Flight 3411. In an interview with the *Washington Post* the same day United issued its *Action Report*, United's CEO admitted: "Our review shows that many things went wrong that day, but the headline is clear: our policies got in the way of our values and procedures interfered in doing what's right."[4]

Testifying before Congress a few weeks later, United's president offered a slight variation on the CEO's assessment: "In an industry like ours, safety is always our top priority, and rules are critical to ensuring a safe operation. But in this instance, where safety wasn't the issue, we let rules and operating procedures stand in the way of common sense."[5]

Failure to do "what's right" and failure to exercise "common sense" were two ways of United saying the same thing: Staff didn't know what practices to follow or precisely what management expectations were. At the same time the company was encouraging consumers to "Fly the Friendly Skies" and making promises to provide "a level of service to our customers that makes us a leader in the airline industry," airport personnel had received—or interpreted—management's messages and behaviors to mean that the most important objective was to maximize profit, a message passed along in their response to the challenge of Flight 3411:

- staff intuited the need to get the stranded crew to Louisville was more important than treating passengers professionally,
- using ticket prices to sequence passengers required to deplane emphasized cost as the main factor in decision-making, and
- settling for addressing minor efficiencies (e.g., "eliminating the red tape on lost bags") in the *Action Report* avoided need for serious reevaluation of corporate values.[6]

Fortunately, unlike the rare exceptions like the GM ignition switch saga wherein management purposely engaged in a cover-up, or Flight 3411 wherein management expectations diverged from practices in the field, assignments that professionals deal with on a routine basis rarely involve dilemmas of such magnitude or consequence. Yet, neither are most assignments in business simple, one-dimensional activities.

Assignments may require dealing with organizations that have conflicting schedules, as well as differing resource needs, priorities, performance objectives, and theories. Organizations may also have different risks, differing opportunities, and differing levels of authority. At the same time, pertinent information needed to address assignments may not be apparent or readily accessible.

Moreover, the higher one ascends the corporate ladder, the less direction will be provided regarding how to proceed with an assignment, what specifically constitutes successful completion, how and which organizations may be affected, or with whom to engage.

Accordingly, the onus is on the professional receiving the assignment to proceed appropriately. Doing so requires applying an approach that ensures the challenge has been accurately defined, thoughtfully analyzed, options appropriately prioritized, and the request thoroughly addressed. Anything less is unacceptable and may signal management that the individual is not up to the task and is likely unready to assume greater responsibility. And, even if the ill-equipped professional stumbles upon an acceptable solution, the lack of a disciplined approach diminishes the likelihood of producing a response that merits more than passing acknowledgment of having completed the assignment.

Proceeding with a Sense of Purpose

Although it is readily acknowledged that "purpose ... is all important," there exists a wide range of interpretations as to what is meant when writers speak about "purpose."[7] While originally cast by Aristotle in terms of three categories of argument (arguments presented in defense of individual freedom, discussions of the affairs of government, and eulogies), purpose, as most commonly presented in the literature and communication texts, is either associated with specific modes of discourse (e.g., literary, persuasive) or is presented as if synonymous with the form in which the final product is to appear (e.g., a presentation or a technical report).

However, these representations oversimplify the reality experienced in the business world and tend to yield vague and understated examples of the dimensions, complexity, and urgency of projects that must be negotiated. The consequences potentially arising from misinterpreting the breadth or complexity of an assignment can be arriving at unsatisfactory solutions as well as fostering assumptions about the professional's level of capability.

That is why, to be successful, the process of responding to an assignment in business needs to begin with a careful crafting of the problem statement that declares both the scope of the assignment and the measure of its success. In doing so, care needs to be taken to avoid wording that presupposes a solution, incorrectly limits or overstates the scope of the research, or specifies the presumed corrective actions. Any such statement may misdirect or crimp the analysis and adversely affect the problem's resolution.

As an example, consider a problem statement proposed in response to an increasing number of customer complaints about long lines at a clothing store return counter: "We need to overhaul our procedures for handling returns."

Not only does the statement presuppose that procedures are the exclusive (or even correct) source of the problem, it narrows the scope of the review and preordains corrective actions (i.e., modify procedures) that—unless previously validated as the source of the company's problems—creates the equal likelihood of expending significant effort with limited benefit as it does of achieving a successful remedy. Yet, one more consideration should be factored into the formulation of problem statements: the latitude for introducing creative or unexpected solutions.

For the professional intent on gaining positive recognition for abilities at handling complex problems, a creative answer—a demonstration of initiative and ingenuity—is what differentiates the promotable individual. Successful resolution of assignments is not exclusively a function or consequence of ability or knowledge; rather, success—exceeding management's expectations—is not achieved by predictable answers but by defining a path that broadens the benefits the company derives from the problem's resolution and opens unanticipated opportunities for further process improvements, efficiencies, and financial performance. It is the difference between being credited with a technically correct answer and being praised for a masterful accomplishment and for one's quality of thought. It is this ability, as Albert Einstein pointed out in his book, *The Evolution of Physics*, by which broader, more creative resolutions to problems are discovered:

> *formulation of a problem is often more essential than its solution, which may be merely a matter of mathematical or experimental skills. To raise new questions, new problems, to regard old problems from a new angle, requires creative imagination and marks real advance in science ... seeing known facts in a new light [must] be stressed.*[8]

It is a contention aptly illustrated by a famous anecdote that speaks to this alignment between problem statement and creativity.

A physics instructor challenged students with the following problem: "Show how it is possible to determine the height of a tall building with the aid of a barometer." Expecting discussion of calculating differences in pressure at the base and top of the building, the instructor received one intriguing answer: "Take the barometer to the top of the building, attach a long rope to it, lower the barometer to the street, and then bring it up while measuring the length of the rope. The length of the rope is the height of the building."

Clarifying the assignment, the instructor informed the student that the answer needed to demonstrate a "knowledge of physics." Undaunted, the student offered a second solution: "Take the barometer to the top of the building; lean over the edge of the roof, and then drop the barometer.

Time the fall with a stopwatch and then calculate the height by using the standard formula for calculating distance of a free-falling object ($S = 1/2at^2$)." Following several more unconventional answers, the student admitted she knew the expected answer but thought it more interesting to consider alternatives. Conceding the student's responses were, in fact, "aided" by a barometer and did demonstrate a knowledge of physics, the instructor acknowledged the student had "completely and correctly" answered the problem.[9]

Although in this case, the intent was obviously to solicit an answer about differences in barometric pressure, both the initial and rewording of the problem statement allowed for more than just the anticipated or traditional answers. While we can expect all the students to have had correct answers, only one student stood out.

In this instance, the number of potentially correct answers results from reliance on a vague formulation of the problem. At its most fundamental level, an equivalent mistake in business to that made by the physics instructor would be assuming that a simple-sounding request (e.g., the request to provide management with a project update) merely requires validation the project is still on schedule, when in fact the expected response may entail a complete assessment of current and anticipated financial and schedule performance, an evaluation of the safety controls, or even a determination regarding the effectiveness of management.

A good share of the practice of defining the problem, of course, derives from experience with similar requests, familiarity with the manager's scope of responsibility, and the relevant credentials you bring to the assignment. In that regard, as a first step in the process of determining the breadth of an assignment and the types of information needed, Table 1.1 offers a list of questions that might warrant consideration—recognizing that the more proficient one becomes with the process, the less need for a question-by-question assessment. With that expectation in mind, Table 1.1 is designed to accommodate two additional levels of sophistication in the discovery process.

As a first step in transitioning from a question-by-question fashioning of a research plan to a more targeted analysis, professionals can construct lines of inquiry based on the five phases of business assignments (shown in the second column of Table 1.1):

- Receiving the Assignment: examining why the individual was chosen,
- Understanding the Assignment: grasping the context of the assignment,
- Researching the Assignment: identifying primary information sources,
- Analyzing Data/Defining the Answer: positing and testing solutions,
- Planning the Presentation: structuring the reporting out to management.

Further advancing the process of conducting data gathering and research, professionals can (as shown in the far-left column of Table 1.1) aggregate

Table 1.1 Gaining Insight into the Assignment

	Gaining Perspective on the Assignment	
	Phase of the Assignment	Primary Questions to Answer
Influencing Constituents	**Receiving the Assignment**	1 What precisely have I been asked to do? 2 Why specifically was I selected for this assignment? 3 Was I given initial indication of what constitutes a successful solution?
	Understanding the Assignment	4 Why is it important to undertake this assignment at this time? 5 What is the corporate significance of the assignment? 6 How does this activity align with corporate policies and values? 7 Is the assignment part of any ongoing (or previous) reviews or initiatives? 8 Who originated the assignment? 10 Is the assignment unique in any way from other recent assignments? 11 To whom am I accountable for any interim/final reporting? 12 How will my response be used, by whom, and when?
Informing Clients	**Researching the Assignment**	13 What fundamental issues (underlying values) are associated with the assignment? 14 Are there interrelated issues that may affect acceptance of particular solutions? 15 Are there precedents or previously determined positions regarding the issues? 16 Which organizations do I need to involve in the review? 17 What documents or corporate resources do I need to examine? 18 What external resources do I need to review?
	Analyzing the Data/Defining the Answer	19 What is the extent of the problem and extent of impact? 20 Have I considered all reasonable alternatives/and all perspectives? 21 Are there creative solutions/options? 22 Is the selected solution implementable given known limitations (e.g., resources)? 23 To what degree can the proposed solution be tested? 24 Does the solution have other applications? 25 Are there lessons learned that need to be shared?
	Planning the Presentation	26 What form is the response intended to take (e.g., report, letter, presentation)? 27 Are there different forms of presentations for affected organizations? 28 What corporate guidance exists regarding language and terminology? 29 Are there specific review and approval requirements? 30 Are there examples of specific formatting requirements?

lines of inquiry into two broad information categories: Informing Clients and Influencing Constituents.

Informing Clients establish the exact dimensions and context of the assignment. Stepping beyond the explicitly articulated expectations that management may have provided when making the assignment, these factors reflect the corporate circumstances, cultural factors, and organizational concerns that circumscribe the dimensions of the assignment. As such, Informing Clients addresses the "what" of the communication project.

On the other side of the equation, representative of the argument's underlying assumptions, Influencing Constituents capture the "why" of the assignment, concentrating on the dynamic considerations—the variables—at play that comprise the universe in which the assignment exists.

An Exercise on Purpose

Having established the scope and context of the assignment along with the sources of information, attention turns to the research, analysis, and, ultimately the formulation of the final solution. Figure 1.1 is a summary-level depiction of the entire assignment process.

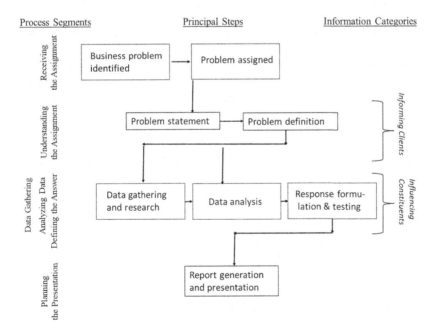

Figure 1.1 Putting the Assignment Process in Perspective.

The Assignment

To allow a recognizable context to this process of developing a proper response to a complex business problem and to provide a practical discussion of strategy and techniques, we will illustrate the process using an actual assignment received in the early days of my management career.

A major corporation in which I managed several small administrative functions was anticipating an extended period of potentially reduced funding. The company, a major international enterprise, occupied a site encompassing several square miles, employed several thousand people, and essentially operated as a self-contained city. Scattered about the site, functions included administrative and business organizations, research and laboratory operations, production facilities, production support activities (e.g., warehousing, maintenance, industrial safety, utilities), multi-million-dollar construction projects, and general site support facilities (e.g., training centers, security stations, fire stations).

In a management meeting with the vice president of our division, we were informed a cost-savings initiative was being undertaken in advance of anticipated budget restrictions. Whereas many people assumed the initiative would focus on staffing reductions, instead, the intent of the initiative, as explained by the vice president, was to identify sufficient cost savings to negate the need for staffing cuts.

At the same time, not wanting to expend great effort with minimal payback, management set two criteria for the effort: (1) selected initiatives had to produce at least $1 million in savings over the next two to three years, and (2) initiatives could not adversely affect production commitments.

My assignment coming out of a subsequent meeting with my immediate management was to determine if copier leasing might offer the desired magnitude of savings. The assignment—derived from an impression the vice president had shared with my manager that "copiers were everywhere"—came with no specific information or guidance, just an impression. Owing to that impression, I now had 60 days after which I, like others similarly assigned, was scheduled to present my conclusions to the company leadership.

Given the briefing provided by the vice president, the assignment started off with a clear statement of the problem, the context of the assignment, and the company's definition of success:

Problem Statement	In 60 days, detail the potential savings that can be realized from the budget for leased copiers,
Context	The company was committed to offset anticipated budget shortfalls,
Expectation	Identify savings, if feasible, in excess of $1 million to be realized over the course of no more than the next 3 fiscal years.

With this definition of the assignment established, efforts shifted to a focus on data collection.

Analysis and Solution

Administered by the property organization, copier management had active leases for more than 100 copiers that were located in essentially every occupied facility on the site. Most of the original copier placements had been done years earlier, with minimal subsequent attention paid to maintaining alignment of copier usage and capability: Copier placements ignored major organizational changes, relocation of functions, adjustments in staffing levels, and operational changes related to scopes of work and regulatory responsibilities—all factors affecting copying needs and services.

The first question to be answered was whether the total annual costs of copier leases were substantial enough to make achieving the savings threshold ($1 million) feasible. Reviewing invoices and contracts determined that the average annual leasing budget for each of the previous two years was $1.5 million; actual expenses averaged $1.3 million. Without much room for margin, reaching the required savings threshold was going to be extremely challenging.

Arriving at a quick yet accurate determination of potential savings required identification of information sources that were most immediately relevant, accessible, and manageable within the assignment's time constraints. In this instance those criteria translated into a combination of documents, records, and discussions:

- company strategic plans to identify current and anticipated facility staffing levels and anticipated organizational relocations;
- discussions with building managers and copier custodians regarding copier placement, constraints (e.g., space, power, networks), as well as capabilities and capacities needed;
- leasing contracts to gain a history of copier usage, performance, age, and total costs for individual units and models (page charges, supplies, servicing, repairs, relocations);
- industry literature to determine recommended models and alternatives available to meet individual facility needs (e.g., multiple paper sizes, color printing, security, networking, speed, and anticipated volumes).

As this resource list might suggest, the volume of information generated (abbreviated in Table 1.2) was quite extensive. Moreover, it was becoming growingly apparent that the complexity of individually dealing with more than 100 copiers and dozens of facilities was beyond the breadth of what might be accomplished in the limited time available. Most

Table 1.2 Summary of Information Gathered

Current Cost/Unit and Annual	*$300–$900 Monthly Per Copier; Total Cost ~$1.3 Million Per Year*
How many?	144 leased copiers; 26 owned desktop printers and copiers
Where they are?	• 3 Office Buildings • 3 Production/manufacturing facilities • 32 Fixed-position office trailers • 6 Construction trailers (relocated as needed) • 8 Special functional buildings(e.g., security/maintenance shops) • 1 Research center
Average Usage levels?	58 within 10% of monthly rating; 86 significantly (>25%) greater or less than recommended volume Copier selection had been established at facilities using occupancy rates (both actual and projected) indicated in the company's 2008 strategic plan
Leased vs. Owned?	6 copiers used for classified work are owned; all others, with exception of 26 desktop printers/copiers are leased
Leasing contracts	80 leased copiers are all full service (maintenance included) Segment 5/6 copiers include click charges that apply above certain volumes Duration remaining on leases range from 4 months to 3 years
Models/Age?	With limited exceptions, all leased machines are recent models Desktop printers remaining lifetimes estimated as 3–5 years Most copiers had been in their current placements for at least 8 years
Capabilities Required?	100 copiers are networked—scanning/faxing/secure printing /email capable 20 of networked copiers also provide color printing 40 copiers are standalone black and white only
Classified/Unclassified work?	All but 6 owned copiers are used for unclassified work only
Ease of Access by building personnel?	Locations within facilities had been assigned when the original lease was signed; the vast majority had not been re-evaluated
Anticipated changes in building occupancies?	With exception of construction trailers, all locations, functional assignments, and occupancy levels were considered to be stable for the near term
Supply costs?	Differ from model to model; estimated annual budget set at $168,000/year
Special requirements?	Information protection (secure copying) critical in organizations with sensitive information—Human Resources/Finance/Procurement/Legal

significantly the mound of information was drawing attention away from the goal of achieving savings.

What was needed was a new problem statement, one that would appropriately cause the challenge to be regarded from "a new angle." Rather than trying to fix 100 individual problems, the problem statement needed to encompass a broader perspective. As such, the new problem statement was developed to set out a more expansive, more creative, and more demanding challenge:

What change of a magnitude and consequence in the copier management program could result in >$1 million in savings?

The answer was immediate: Design the copier program as if we currently had none. Rather than attempting to resolve dozens of issues at each facility, the information already collected would form the substance of an entirely new plan. Freed from the enormous complexity of the original approach, the new strategy raised the perspective to a manageable, implementable level—one that would also more readily allow for the quantification of potential savings.

In this new plan, on a facility-by-facility basis, copiers would be assigned, and their placement determined, using six factors:

- average monthly copier volume (total pages) at each facility over the past year (plus adding a 5% allowance to accommodate fluctuations in use);
- selecting copiers with sufficient speed to produce the determined monthly volume assuming machines were being used an average of 3 hours a day (the average time cited in industry literature);
- identifying machines that in addition to the necessary speed and volume ratings provided the capabilities identified during the information-gathering process (e.g., networking, scanning, color printing, output sizes, secure copying);
- placement options (e.g., availability of power, network connections);
- the estimated number of building occupants requiring routine copying services; and
- availability (nearby placement) of additional, alternate copying capability in the event of machine downtime or need for periodic additional capability.

As detailed in Table 1.3, applying this set of factors resulted in a significant proposed recasting of copier leasing for the company. Not only did the cost savings exceed the $1 million threshold for a three-year period: The new plan better-aligned capability with need and minimized resource commitments from other organizations required to assist in its implementation.

Table 1.3 Recasting the Copier Program

Savings Potential: $559,600 Per Year

Facility	Copier Placement Pre-analysis					Implemented Copier Initiative				
	Copier Segment*					Copier Segment				
	6	5	3 & 4	2	Desk	6	5	3 & 4	2	Desk
Office Buildings	0	18	18	0	9	0	18	0	0	0
Permanent trailer villages	0	15	60	0	8	0	0	20	12	8
Non-permanent office trailers	0	0	6	6	6	0	0	6	0	6
Special operations (e.g., classified operations)	0	0	4	0	2	0	0	4	0	2
Production support	0	0	3	3	2	0	0	4	0	6
Security/Powerhouses	0	0	2	3	2	0	0	3	0	7
Research Facilities	0	2	6	0	0	0	2	4	0	0
Bldg 1 Manned Copy Center	2	0	0	0	0	0	0	0	0	0
Total	2	33	97	12	29	0	20	41	12	29
Net Change						-2	-13	-56		
Annual Savings ($ Thousands)**						$90 ***	$93.6	$336		
						Estimated Savings on Supplies: $40				

Notes

* Copier Segment 1 = 15–20 pages per minute (ppm); 2 = 21–30; 3 = 31–40; 4= 41–69; 5= 70–90; 6= 91+

** Savings based on average monthly costs: Segment 1=$200; 2=$300; 3=$500; 4=$600; 5= $750; 6=$900

*** Copy center savings represent eliminating two Segment 6 copiers and reassigning the copier clerk

Table 1.4 Establishing the Priority of Themes

Statement of Assignment: Determine Potential Savings from Copier Leases

Presentation Theme	Priority	Essential
Avoid adverse impacts on commitments	2	√
Minimize implementation resources	6	
Save $1 million	1	√
Achieve savings within 3 years	3	√
Simplify copier management administration	7	
Provide peripheral opportunities (e.g., standardizing supplies)	6	
Improve operational efficiency	4	√
Ensure redundant capability available in the event of copier protracted downtime	5	

In readying the presentation to senior leadership, a simple matrix assisted with assessing and prioritizing potential themes as well as differentiating between the factors with the most significant role in successfully achieving the goals of the assignment from those evaluated areas, although important, that didn't need to be addressed in the presentation owing to time limitations, complexity, or being of limited consequence to the majority of meeting attendees (Table 1.4).

At the same time that these main themes were being defined and prioritized, the revised strategy highlighted several additional near-term and strategic enhancements and cost savings:

- the need for the manned copying center in the administrative building mainly used for small volume copying jobs could be eliminated;
- copying contracts could be established with local printers to handle large volume copying and provide additional capabilities (e.g., professional binding of reports issued to stakeholders);
- copier models in each segment could be standardized, reducing supply costs and improving property administration;
- biennial reviews of copier usage and needs could be conducted to ensure continued alignment among costs, capability, and usage; and
- other administrative functions (e.g., Information Technology) could use the methodology and templates developed in the copier analysis.

Putting the Final Pieces Together

With the solution finalized and the savings quantified, there remained one major area of the presentation to develop. As identified in Table 1.4, there were four themes that needed to be presented to corporate leadership: total

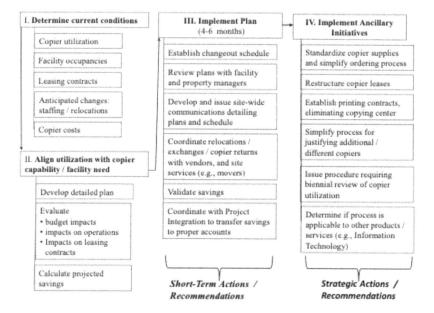

Figure 1.2 The Substance of the Presentation.

savings, avoidance of adverse impacts, timely accomplishment of savings, and enhanced operational efficiency. Meeting all four objectives in the presentation to the corporate leadership required that the demonstration of savings had to be accompanied by a straightforward and practical implementation plan.

That implementation plan (Figure 1.2), which required both management endorsement and engagement, had to be designed to meet a demanding component of any assignment if it was to be successful.

As we will discuss in Chapter 2, to be successful, it is not enough to deliver a proposal to management, the real success derives from delivering a product that makes management's job easy.

Notes

1   "Questions, Answers, and Perspectives on the Current State of Airline Travel," U.S. Congress, Senate, Committee on Commerce, Science, and Transportation, 115th Congress, 1st session, May 4, 2017, https://www.govinfo.gov/content/pkg/CHRG-115shrg28641/html/CHRG-115shrg28641.htm

2   Susan Carey, "United Says Litany of Failures Led to Flight Fiasco: Dragging of Passenger David Dao from Plane, CEO Oscar Munoz Says Was 'A Failure of Epic Proportions … We Get It,' *Wall Street Journal*, April 27, 2017.

3   Eric Sigurdson, "Corporate Leadership and Culture: United Airlines & the 'Re-Accommodated' Doctor – Guiding Principles for Boards, C-Suite Executives, and General Counsel," *Sigurdson Post*, May 2017, http://www.sigurdsonpost.com/2017/05/02/corporate-leadership-and-culture-united-airlines-the-re-accommodated-doctor-guiding-principles-for-boards-c-suite-executives-and-general-counsel.

4   Sigurdson, "Corporate Leadership and Culture."

5   "Questions, Answers, and Perspectives."

6   United Airlines, "United Express Flight 3411 *Review and Action Report*," April 27, 2016, http://viewfromthewing.com/wp-content/uploads/2017/04/United-Flight-3411-Review-and-Action-Report.pdf.

7   Nancy Roundy Blyler, "Purpose and Composition Theory: Issues in the Research," *Journal of Advanced Composition* 9, no. 1/2 (1989): 100.

8   Albert Einstein, *The Evolution of Physics: Form Early Concepts to Relativity and Quanta* (New York: Simon and Schuster, 1966), 92.

9   Alexander Calandra, "Angels on a Pin," *Saturday Review,* December 21, 1968, 60.

Chapter 2

Making Management's Job Easy

Poor decisions are a consequence of one of four factors: (1) information provided was insufficient or inaccurate; (2) information was disregarded; (3) information was never received; or (4) information that should have been required was not provided. All four of these conditions played a role in the sinking of British Petroleum's (BP) Deepwater Horizon oil rig, and, in the words of President Obama, in triggering "the worst environmental disaster America has ever faced."[1]

Yet, BP's first decision regarding drilling in the Gulf of Mexico's Mississippi Canyon was particularly prescient. Having secured oil rights to a drilling tract 49 miles off the Louisiana coast, BP dubbed its newly acquired site "Macondo," naming it after the fictional town in Gabriel Garcia Marquez's novel, *One Hundred Years of Solitude*. As if presaging Deepwater Horizon's fate, the two Macondo's shared an existence signified by extremely fluctuating fortunes:

> *It was as if God had decided to put to the test every capacity for surprise and was keeping the inhabitants of Macondo in a permanent alternation between excitement and disappointment, doubt and revelation, to such an extreme that no one knew for certain where the limits of reality lay.*[2]

Beginning modestly, initial oil drilling in the ocean had begun using wells anchored to the shore by wooden piers. Advancing further ashore, in 1938, a drill rig positioned a mile-and-a-half from the Louisiana shoreline in 14 feet of water became the first free-standing ocean unit to produce oil. Technology soon made routine drilling possible in "shallow" waters (up to 250-foot depths) and, not long after, in "ultra-deepwater," depths greater than 1000 feet.

By the beginning of the 21st century, BP leases in the Gulf accounted for approximately one-third of all known deepwater reserves. When the original drill rig at Macondo was damaged by Hurricane Ida, Deepwater Horizon, an

DOI: 10.4324/9781003455585-3

ultra-deepwater rig with unrivaled safety and production records, replaced it. Built at a cost of $350 million and costing $1 million per day to lease, Deepwater Horizon resumed the drilling, which already reached 9,000 feet below the ocean's surface—4,000 feet of it below the seabed. Another 9,000 feet remained for Deepwater Horizon to reach the oil and gas reservoir. However, poor decision-making owing to a range of information-related and communication issues precluded ever finishing the job.

Drilling had begun with a handicap: Safety had been overtaken by a government drive for revenues. Originally intending to secure the Gulf as a Naval Petroleum Reserve, the federal government placed a moratorium on drilling outside a three-mile radius of the coast. However, oil embargoes and the allure of substantial revenues reversed that decision, leading to the auctioning of hundreds of Gulf tracts.

At the same time, tracts in the central and western portions of the Gulf were exempted from existing safety requirements and from much of the National Environmental Policy Act—eliminating need for rigorous safety assessments in advance of drilling. Further diminishing the quality of operating and engineering decisions, the Minerals Management Service, the agency charged with oversight of offshore drilling—understaffed and underfunded—was prevented from issuing safety rules. "Thus [the government] never achieved [oversight] consonant with practices that most other countries had embraced decades earlier"; drilling operators, in turn, never were fully accountable to demonstrate that decisions adequately addressed safety.[3]

Yet, weakened oversight and relief from safety controls were only two of several factors contributing to poor decision-making. As highlighted by the Presidential Commission examining Deepwater Horizon, "The most significant failure[s] at Macondo ... can be traced back to underlying failures of management and communication"—and, more specifically, to BP's decision-making processes and protocols.[4] Those failures began at the top, with corporate's lack of engagement in decision-making: None of the three people with corporate accountability for Deepwater Horizon's operation (not the CEO, the chief executive for exploration, nor the chief operating officer for exploration) had been "following the activities on the drilling rig."[5]

Evidenced in practices on the oil rig, this undisciplined decision-making, as one senator characterized it, was indicative of "a culture that evolved over the years that seemed to ignore risk, tolerate non-compliance, and accepted incompetence." It was, as the senator pointed out, BP accepting and condoning BP "violating its own policies."[6]

One factor, as was the case with GM, was compartmentalizing information: BP did not share information with its contractors (or sometimes with its crew); contractors, in turn, did not share information with BP or with each other. As the commission noted, "individuals often found themselves making critical decisions without a full appreciation for the context in which they were being made (or even without recognition that the decisions were critical)."[7]

Three examples of these breakdowns should suffice to make evident the magnitude and breadth of information-related problems hampering effective decision-making:

- Well design changes appeared "to have been made by the BP Macondo team in ad hoc fashion without any formal risk analysis or internal expert review."[8]
- Applicable industry lessons were ignored. One ignored lesson from a companion BP rig identified anomalous pressure readings akin to those on Deepwater Horizon the day of the explosion were linked to a potentially catastrophic blowout—an uncontrollable release of oil and gas.
- BP routinely issued unreviewed and unapproved procedures without any input from or training provided to affected staff.

Although those three examples provide a general sense of communication and decision-making shortcomings, two ill-informed decisions contributed directly to Deepwater Horizon's demise:

- Personnel cementing well sections together were not informed that the cement had failed an integrity test, suggesting potential for an impending well failure.
- BP's design specified use of 16 centralizers to guide cement placement when sealing well segments together; however, only six were available. Although alternative units were purchased, engineering, without further analysis or consultation, authorized work to proceed using just the six originally available centralizers.

Together, reliance on subpar-quality cement and insufficient sealing of the well's lining, diminished the well's engineering and operating integrity. On April 20, 2010, at 9:49 p.m., a blowout occurred. The gas and oil spewing from the well ignited, exploded, and, within a matter of hours, sank Deepwater Horizon.

Defining Information Needs

The most fundamental approach often cited in business communication texts as the means of defining information needs is by considering demographic factors about the "audience." This demographic approach presumably provides insights regarding the type and volume of information the "audience" needs, as well as providing guidance on the structuring of communications. In addition to resulting in an insufficient assessment of applicable information, more significantly, relying on this approach is likely to result in faulty assumptions about and flimsy responses to the assignment for two principal reasons:

1 The concept of audience as a homogenous gathering of people rarely applies when providing information needed for making decisions within a business context. With exception of such situations as addressing a group of customers or a shareholder meeting, the broader the business audience, the greater the probability individuals have diverse interests, differing intended applications for the information, and differing opinions as to the significance of the information.

2 Demographics offer no meaningful correspondence to management's or colleagues' assignments, responsibilities, or professional performance. At most, some personal details may have minimal bearing on the selection or tailoring of a communication, but certainly not nearly enough insight on which to risk one's reputation by submitting an incomplete or poorly framed response to an assignment.

Rather, prudent decision-making in business is only possible with a full appreciation that every business involves a dynamic environment in which unique systems have been implemented for making decisions and controlling the flow of information.

The Information Environment

As opposed to demographics' highly generalized and speculative approach to defining information needs, professionals need to have and employ a fundamental understanding of the unique framework and governance of the company for the resolution of complex assignments.

Assignments to junior personnel are often tightly governed by very prescriptive company protocols and procedures—in terms of both the process to be followed as well as the expected form and substance; these junior personnel are not necessarily expected to understand the assignment's implications or the avenues warranting pursuit. The exact opposite is expected of more senior staff—and is also commonly reflected in assignments given to professionals being considered for potential advancement.

These more complex assignments—with limited established pathways—demand tailored, individualized, and unique communication strategies predicated on a thorough appreciation of the workings and design of the corporate organization. Making management's job easy in these circumstances is accomplished by delivering a product that, beyond meriting endorsement, responds to the full complement of affected organizations, is well reasoned and practical, and—as we noted in Chapter 1—demonstrates initiative, ingenuity, and creativity.

Arriving at this quality of response relies on the ability to align the solution with the culture of the company—its structural design, distribution of decision-making authorities, and the controls maintaining coordination among functions and organizations. It is the recognition of and adapting responses to these interwoven company attributes that define the total scope of the assignment, its breadth of implications and ramifications, and the communication strategies critical to gaining acceptance and authorization to implement the solution.

Fundamentals of Corporate Structuring

Although there are numerous means by which to classify and categorize corporate structures and their approaches to defining information pathways and assigning authority for decision-making, there is a fundamental, common denominator that underpins all companies.

As succinctly articulated in the introduction to Henry Mintzberg's *The Structuring of Organization*, at the most fundamental level, all corporations are designed around two components: Segregating work into distinct functions or programs and then establishing the means by which to maintain appropriate coordination among them:

> *Every organized human activity—from the making of pots to the placing of a man on the moon—gives rise to two fundamental and opposing requirements: the division of labor into various tasks to be performed and the coordination of these tasks to accomplish the activity. The structure of an organization can be defined simply as the sum of the ways in which it divides its labor into distinct tasks and then achieves coordination among them.[9]*

This division of tasks and coordination among them, as Mintzburg explains, is accomplished through a complex and integrated alignment among the strategies and mechanisms companies employ to promote active information sharing, assign routine decision-making authority, and maintain performance standards. And, for us, it is understanding these inter-relationships that holds the key to fashioning tailored communications that gain endorsement and promote individual recognition as a result of having made management's job easy.

Basics of Corporate Decision-Making

Demonstrating how the two elements (segregating tasks and coordinating among them) work, Mintzberg goes on to explain the five corporate communities and their respective authorities and scopes of responsibility:

- The "strategic apex" represents the senior management who define the company's mission and vision and who establish the company's operating philosophy and corporate policies;
- The "technostructure" comprises personnel (e.g., engineers, accountants) who establish the procedures and protocols, define performance standards, and ensure compliance;
- The "middle line" is made up of all remaining levels of supervision, with responsibility for facility- and functional-level decisions regarding personnel, risks, budgets, schedules, and resource allocations;
- The "support staff" are personnel providing day-to-day ancillary services central to sustaining effective operation of the company (e.g., maintenance, security, legal counsel);
- The "operative core" constitutes the front line, the personnel who produce and deliver the company's products and services (e.g., machinists, assembly line personnel, sales personnel).

As example of this corporate structure, we might consider a city school system. In that system, the district superintendent functions as the strategic apex with the district offices (the technostructure) promulgating instructional policy. The middle line is performed by principals and vice principals, with bus drivers, administrative staff, and food workers functioning as support staff. Teachers, charged with "delivering" education, constitute the operative core. (Of course, in small corporate enterprises, there may not be five distinct communities, as would be the case in a store with only one level of management representing both the strategic apex and the technostructure.)

Implementing the company's mission and maintaining the integrity of its value system is principally accomplished through assigning decision-making authority—delegating responsibility for minimizing potential risks, establishing short-term goals, making commitments, and implementing organizational changes. As such, it is this assignment of decision-making authority by which a company principally announces and maintains its culture.

That delegation, which begins at the level of the Strategic Apex, can be extensive or limited, centralized or decentralized, extended through horizontal components of a single functional organization, or extended vertically through successive levels of management and professionals.

Decision-making can also be accomplished by a combination of horizontal and vertical delegations within a single function of the organization. This would be the case, for instance, if a procurement manager who is given authority for all subcontracting, in turn, delegates full authority for individual subcontracts to the department procurement leads.

These decisions send clear signals regarding both the company's operating philosophy and the intended relationship among the five communities. Assigning authority to the technostructure or to the support staff announces the company's intent to increase standardization of operations and intent to strengthen governance. Or, if issues are impeding meeting production quotas, senior management (the Strategic Apex) may assign the operative core increased decision-making authority, giving production functions full latitude to realign schedules, adjust budgets, and reallocate resources among multiple support organizations. Whatever alignments among communities are instituted, controls are needed to maintain the integrity of activities.

The Composition of Standardization

As we witnessed with operation of Deepwater Horizon, failures by at least four of the communities (Strategic Apex, Middle Line, Technostructure, and Operative Core) occurred. The corporate officers, rig management, engineering staff, and work crews all failed to adhere to the standards established and the expected responsibilities for which they were authorized. Rather than promoting the corporation's mission and value in the performance of their duties ("Our goal [is] no accidents, no harm to people and no damage to the environment"), universal dismissal of prescribed controls, protocols, and lines of authority resulted in the loss of 11 lives, an uncontrolled release of more than 200 million gallons of crude oil into the Gulf, the beginning of a sustained environmental calamity stretching across more than 600 miles of coastal shoreline, and the near demise of BP.[10]

Although a well-documented organizational framework was in place, with explicit authorities and decision-making authority established, Deepwater Horizon experienced persistent deviations from the prescribed methods for conducting work: ignoring engineering specifications (e.g., proceeding with too few centralizers); failure to act consistent with training (e.g., not challenging anomalous pressure readings); and a disregard for safety and quality control rules (e.g., ignoring lessons learned).

Protecting against these types of misadventure, companies rely on three forms of controls: specific task-related controls that ensure the adequacy, consistency, and efficiency of processes; controls that ensure personnel maintain the requisite capabilities and knowledge to conduct work safely and efficiently; and controls that ensure a consistent quality, quantity, and timeliness of the products and services produced by the company.

Individually, a few deviations from these standards and controls—although unacceptable—may be accommodated and mitigated by other interlocked controls within the system. However, when widespread, when systemic deviations persist in process, training, or output, they eventually translate into failures: the lack of accountability underpinning the GM ignition switch fiasco, the unprofessional management of Flight 3411, or the loss of operational integrity aboard Deepwater Horizon.

Process Standardization

Most commonly, process standardization occurs in the form of procedures for conducting routine daily activities, and, often, denoting what to do in response to non-routine circumstances. At nuclear power plants, for instance, control rooms have libraries containing three different sets of procedures: normal operating procedures for administering routine operations; alarm response procedures, that, as the name makes evident, are used when indicators announce that readings are outside prescribed operating ranges; and emergency procedures, detailing immediate actions to mitigate or remedy situations that might otherwise result in significant safety issues or system failures.

A similar form of hierarchical procedural control exists in most businesses and industries. Depending on the complexity of the work and the risks associated with doing activities incorrectly, procedural controls may be simple verbal directions or may encompass a cascading hierarchy extending corporate policies applicable to all employees down to detailed desk instructions used exclusively by clerks handling paperwork.

Skills Standardization

Complementing procedures in delivering on the corporately intended practices regarding decision-making and information flow, training ensures compliance by translating policy into individual work assignments. And, as Deepwater Horizon demonstrated, the safety and operational integrity of the company demands a tailored flow of information that ensures every employee has the appropriate skills to carry out the physical tasks of the work assignment as well as the knowledge of the interplay between that set of responsibilities and the functions that precede and follow it in the process of delivering on company commitments.

As a single example that suggests how crimping the flow of information between interfacing functions leads to lapses in decision-making and failures in fulfilling responsibilities, we need only to consider one of the two critical factors contributing to the demise of Deepwater Horizon that we cited earlier: the use of sub-standard cement.

Had thorough training been in place, the engineers—as directed in specifications and procedures—would have taken immediate steps to preclude further use of the cement, notified management of the test results, contacted operations to initiate remediating actions had any of the cement already been released for use, and formed an assessment team to determine a path forward. And, even had engineering failed to take those appropriate actions, the crew pouring the cement should have acted on training that required suspending further pours pending further authority from senior management.

If the proper notifications had been made upon determining out-of-specification results, had the engineers or cement crew made the decisions as directed in procedures and training, and had the lessons learned from the sister rig that had experienced similar cement readings been implemented, Deepwater Horizon, its crew, and the company reputation would have been saved. However, the confluence of the failures to communicate, as cited in the Commission report referenced earlier, left personnel on Deepwater Horizon making consequential decisions without "appreciation ... [or] recognition that the decisions were critical."

Output Standardization

Consistently delivering a quality product—whether considering products being delivered from one individual or one function to another within the company or those products or services produced by the company—relies on standardization of processes and skills. Confirming that those skills are dutifully applied falls to a third set of controls governing outputs.

Lacking rigorous oversight of internal processes and performance as was the case with disengaged corporate management responsible for Deepwater Horizon allowed for all the failings: Violations of procedures and engineering specifications; cabining of information; poor quality control; and deviations from established responsibilities and authorities. Although the range of failures was significant, in the end, it was the lack of oversight—the implicit acceptance of a situation out of control—that doomed Deepwater Horizon.

As is the case with the other sets of control (process and skills), the amount and form of oversight, along with the frequency at which it is applied, must be commensurate with the scope and complexity of the operation being monitored. For instance, had management focused oversight on determining whether the engineering department was consistently compliant with specifications but had not been equally assertive in reviewing the practices used by the teams pouring cement, it would not have concluded there was a widespread systemic failure that required attention to the platform's local and corporate management. Reaching that conclusion would have required a more comprehensive oversight program.

Using Corporate Logic to Make Management's Job Easy

This understanding of the organizational attributes—flow of information, delegation of authority, responsibility for, decision-making, and administration of controls—poses the basis for responding to complex communication challenges. That process involves two principal steps: Defining the unique information needs of affected personnel or functions and the communication strategy to deliver that information.

To provide a practical illustration of these two steps, we'll return to our Chapter 1 assignment to determine and then present the company leadership with a plan for achieving potential savings from analysis of the copier leasing program.

Primary Tailoring

That assignment began with direction that included a preliminary problem statement, the context, and a definition of success: Namely, to avoid company layoffs, in 60 days a presentation was to be provided to the company leadership team addressing the feasibility of saving at least $1 million within the next three years from the administration of leased copiers.

Research and analysis had concluded that significant financial recovery was feasible and, in anticipation of the scheduled presentations, both a set of themes and an implementation plan had been drafted for use in the presentation. However, although the research, themes, and implementation plan constitute the substance of the presentation, the strategy for employing these components to secure leadership's endorsement for the proposal had not yet been formulated. That formulation calls for adapting the material to align it to the structure of the company and the mechanisms it used to "achieve coordination."

In specific, the development and tailoring of a persuasive presentation attuned to the corporate structure and governance logic requires melding the four-part structure of the implementation plan (current configuration, proposed configuration, implementation, and benefits) and the presentation themes consistent with the logic of how the company "divides its labor into distinct tasks and then achieves coordination among them." That synthesis is the means to define the critical information needs of each member of the leadership team, and the most appropriate means for its delivery (Table 2.1).

Table 2.1 Defining the Substance of the Senior Staff Presentation

Meeting Attendees	Level of Interest in Themes					
	Savings Achieved	Timing of Savings	Avoiding Impacts	Limited Resources Needed	Additional Benefits	Redundant Capability
CEO	Major	Major	Minor	Summary	Major	Summary
V.P. Operations	Summary	Summary	Major	Minor	Major	Summary
V.P. Finance	Summary	Summary	Summary	Minor	Summary	Summary
V.P. Engineering	Summary	Summary	Summary	Minor	Summary	Summary
V.P. Human Resources	Summary	Summary	Summary	Minor	Summary	Summary
V.P. Business & Administration	Summary	Summary	Summary	Major	Major	Summary
V.P. Safety	Summary	Summary	Summary	Minor	Summary	Summary
General Counsel	Summary	Summary	Summary	Minor	Summary	Minor
Placement in Presentation	Combined Sections 1 & 2: Current and new configuration		Section 3 Implementation		Section 4: Benefits	
Relative Time Allotment	60%		30%		10%	

What this preliminary analysis also makes evident is that there is not a single, homogeneous expectation regarding the subjects of primary interest or the level of information specificity commonly shared among attendees. There is not, to return to our earlier discussion, any such thing as a uniform or single "audience."

Rather, gaining the endorsement for the proposed plan and the acknowledgment of the creativity and accomplishment requires a sufficiently robust communication strategy that gains individual approval from each attendee. Although these individuals will be assembled at the time the official endorsement is solicited, the actual endorsement and approval, for many of the attendees, may be the result of individualized communication strategies that are initiated in advance of the presentation.

Ancillary Tailoring

The challenge that must be answered is this: What communications, in total, are required so that when the proposal's author enters the conference room, the proposal—whose implications will reverberate throughout the corporation—has the greatest probability of obtaining a universal endorsement to proceed?

Catching the leadership team cold may result in the corollary to the admonition from the book *Who's Going to Run GM?* that we cited in the Introduction: Although a "botched" presentation, as that book asserted, will not soon be forgotten, an unconvincing presentation is very soon forgotten.

What our examination of the anatomy of the corporation has prepared us for is recognition that fulfilling all aspects of this communication challenge must begin well before and, often, extend beyond the presentation. In this instance, multiple communication pathways are required: The goal of making management's job easy does not apply solely to the CEO who initiated the assignment, although that person has the ultimate vote; nor does it apply exclusively to your immediate manager, although that individual is of most immediate consequence to your career.

Because this assignment bears direct relevance to every director attending the presentation and relies on a significant degree of their support for its successful implementation, individualized attention is needed in advance of the presentation to ensure each director's job has been made as easy as feasible—recognition that the benefits to their respective organizations are worth the resource needed for its implementation.

Just as the implementation will reach into the local operations and effect every one of the five communities from Strategic Apex through the Operative Core, the effort to win over support needs to reach into those same levels. Sorting out specifically which organizations to deal with in the limited time in advance of the presentation is identified by answering questions regarding the organization and governance logic we have been examining:

- who are the decision-making authorities whose endorsements are most powerful?
- where in the organization is the best entry point to ensure the argument for the proposal filters up to the director? and
- which functions or organizations will have the greatest concerns about impacts on controls and protocols?

Unlike the senior staff whose authorization will largely focus on savings, reaching out to the individuals and organizations identified by answering these three questions and convincing them of the reasonableness of the proposal is the message that they need to deliver to their respective directors. That set of contacts, the focus and timing of discussions, is as critical as the senior leadership team in gaining support and authorization to implement the proposal.

It is by applying sufficient energy to promoting the proposal from within the directors' respective organizations that the real work of selling the proposal occurs. It is that assurance of a positive balance between effort and benefit brought forward from within their ranks that is most meaningful in informing the senior manager's decisions and is the centerpiece of making management's job easy in a complex assignment of this nature.

To that end, complementing Table 2.1 that presented the framework for dealing directly with the senior staff, Table 2.2 extends the analysis of information, concentrating on the needs at the functional level of the organization. In particular, Table 2.1 concentrates on the most intense interests or issues—the functions that need to be courted and persuaded to ensure directors are encouraged to support the proposal. Also, as shown in the table, in most instances it is critical that these discussions are undertaken in advance of the presentation.

At the same time, it must be recognized that in instances where suppositions about the difficulty of implementation or the magnitude of benefits cannot be reasonably assured or substantiated until after implementation, it may be necessary to defer such arguments pending implementation of the proposal. As the familiar maxim goes, the goal—with the leadership team and with colleagues whose assistance is being solicited—is best to "under promise and over deliver," not the inverse.

In summary, understanding how the corporation's structural component (the five communities) operates, interrelates, and maintains performance are the factors that position professionals accurately to assess and effectively define communication strategies—particularly when tackling

Table 2.2 Pursuing Proposal Buy-In

Directorate and Function	Concern	Focus of Communication	Timing Relative to Presentation
Finance Accounts Payable	• Changes in work volumes; • Policy changes	Timing of implementation will provide for gradual increases in any work volumes No changes should be required to policy or procedures	Pre
Accounting	Changes to General Ledger	No specific accounting changes required New structure consistent with existing ledger	Post
Operations Facility Managers	Dislocation of personnel	Careful coordination will minimize disruption No offices affected; all alternate space is now used for support infrastructure	Pre
Maintenance	Electrical work	With exception of Segment 6 machines, all current wiring is sufficient; no additional circuits will be needed Maintenance will be involved in all decisions that require significant rewiring	Pre
Production Managers	Commitment schedules	Activities will be coordinated to maximize use of planned production downtimes. All activities will be incorporated into current production schedules to ensure visibility	Pre
Business and Administration Contracts Management	Volume of new work	The number of new contracts will be minimal with limited change in the number of vendors	Pre and Post

(Continued)

Table 2.2 (Continued)

Directorate and Function	Concern	Focus of Communication	Timing Relative to Presentation
Project Controls	Impacts on overall cost/schedule performance	Most changes will be limited to changes in model numbers and cost statements in contracts	Pre
		Project control analysts will assist in determining timing for a facility-by-facility change-outs	
		Potential schedule impacts will be coordinated with facility and the production managers	
Small Business Programs	Impact on contractual socioeconomic goals	The additional subcontracts will offer increased opportunity to look for small businesses, veteran- and woman-own businesses	Post
Safety Industrial safety	Worker safety	Physical work will involve only routine activities, and no hazardous work is required.	Pre
Engineering Civil engineering	Changes to design drawings	Because only incidental changes to facility wiring are anticipated, minimal—if any—changes will result in required changes to facility drawings	Post

complex assignments and assignments whose implementation affects multiple organizations.

It is an understanding and an appreciation of the interwoven dimensions of a communication task that differentiate an acceptable response from one that merits professional acknowledgment. It is a demonstration of skills that reflects a capability and level of mastery that separates the talented few from the merely capable and the artful response from a mundane one.

Making management's job easy may not always be easy, but it is a cornerstone of generating recognition, presenting one's capabilities in a positive light, and positioning oneself for advancement.

Notes

1 National Commission on the BP Deepwater Horizon Oil Spill and Offshore Drilling (hereafter National Commission), "Deep Water: The Gulf Oil Disaster and the Future of Offshore Drilling–Report to the President," January 11, 2011, 173.
2 Gabriel Garcia Marquez, *One Hundred Years of Solitude*, trans. Gregory Rambassa (New York: Avon Books, 1970), 212.
3 National Commission, "Deep Water," 71.
4 National Commission, "Deep Water," 122.
5 "Hearing before the Committee on Energy and Natural Resources," U.S. Congress, 112th Cong., 1st sess., January 26, 2011, *National Commission Report on the BP Oil Spill*, Before the Committee on Energy and Natural Resources, 112th Congress, https://www.govinfo.gov/content/pkg/CHRG-112shrg64994/pdf/CHRG-112shrg64994.pdf.
   National Commission," Deep Water."
6 "Hearing before the Committee," 114.
7 National Commission, "Deep Water," 123.
8 National Commission, "Deep Water," 122.
9 Henry Mintzberg, *The Structuring of Organization* (New York: Prentice Hall, 1979).
10 Beyond Petroleum (BP), "BP Sustainability Review 2009," 2010, https://www.bp.com/content/dam/bp/business-sites/en/global/corporate/pdfs/sustainability/archive/archived-reports-and-translations/2009/bp_sustainability_review_2009.pdf.

Chapter 3

Being Quotable

On June 30, 1863, Union and Confederate regiments converged a few miles from the Maryland/Pennsylvania border. The following morning, three days of battle began at Gettysburg. By the end of the first day, the Union troops, driven out of town, had reassembled at and fortified Cemetery Hill directly south of Gettysburg. The second day witnessed successive attacks on the Union's flanks. On July 3, incorrectly assuming the previous day's fighting had led the Union to shift resources from its center to its flanks, General Robert E. Lee ordered a direct, frontal attack. The assault—by 15,000 men on a fortification defended by 6,500 Union soldiers—was to become the turning point in the war.

Following two hours of artillery bombardments by both Confederate and Union cannons, nine brigades of Confederate infantry advanced. Forced to traverse three-quarters of a mile of open ground to reach Cemetery Hill, the Confederates lay vulnerable to cannon and musket fire. Although a handful of men breached the Union line, more than half were killed or wounded; the remainder were in retreat.

After three days and 40,000–50,000 casualties, the battle ended. On July 4, Lee withdrew his army; the Union commander, General George Meade, pursued Lee into Virginia, but, to President Lincoln's consternation, ended the chase shortly after.

Although Lee's surrender at Appomattox remained two years away, seeking to memorialize the victory and the battle's unequaled sacrifice, for $2,475.81 the Governor of Pennsylvania purchased seventeen acres on Cemetery Hill.[1] Then, in cooperation with other governors who fielded armies at Gettysburg, he set out the cemetery design, assigned plots to each state based on number of fallen soldiers, and established the agreements for funding the cemetery's construction.

The remaining task was arranging for the cemetery's consecration and dedication. The governors' selection of a speaker was unanimous: *Edward Everett.*

DOI: 10.4324/9781003455585-4

Everett's credentials were unrivaled: A respected speaker, he had served five terms in Congress before being elected Governor of Massachusetts. Thereafter, in relatively quick succession, Everett served as envoy to Britain under President William Henry Harrison; President of Harvard University; Secretary of State under President Millard Fillmore; and United States Senator. Moreover, the credential that made him an especially appropriate spokesperson for the occasion was that in the years immediately preceding the Civil War, he had become known as one of the staunchest advocates for maintaining the union.

His speech, "The Great Issues Now Before Our Country," had been delivered more than 100 times in the years leading up to the Civil War. And the speech's theme—that the country's choice was now "whether the work of our noble fathers of the revolutionary and constitutional age shall perish or endure"—was echoed from his national platform as vice-presidential candidate on the Constitutional-Union ticket during the 1860 presidential elections.[2]

Accordingly, David Wills, an aide to the governor of Pennsylvania, sent a note to Everett dated September 23, 1863. It read in part: "This burial-ground will be consecrated to this sacred and holy purpose on Thursday, the 23rd day of October next, with appropriate ceremonies, and the several States interested have united in the selection of you to deliver the Oration on that solemn occasion."[3]

In accepting, Everett requested the dedication be rescheduled to allow time for travel and preparation, a request readily approved by the governors. Several weeks later, on November 19, 1863, the new agreed date, the ceremonies were held. Following introductions and a prayer, Everett rose to speak:

Standing beneath this serene sky, overlooking these broad fields now reposing from the labors of the waning year, the mighty Alleghanies dimly towering before us, the graves of our brethren beneath our feet, it is with hesitation that I raise my poor voice to break the eloquent silence of God and Nature.[4]

In keeping with his opinion that "a respectable patriotic oration" should last between an hour and a half and two hours, Everett's speech of more than 13,000 words—spoken without notes—lasted slightly under two hours.[5] Having read Lee's account of the battle in a Virginia newspaper and further informed by local historians, Everett began by chronicling the battle, the casualties, the war, and the valiant efforts of the nurses. Next came his principal emphasis: An impassioned argument for reconciliation, a healing of the union, concluding with a tribute to Gettysburg's "martyr-heroes."

The national response to Everett's oration was overwhelmingly positive, as a single newspaper account attests:

It was a day which can never be forgotten. It will live in the most vivid recollection of the present generation, ... because of Everett's oration .... as your readers ... will agree. But they can form hence no idea of the effect it had upon the vast audience, which listened in almost breathless silence during the nearly two hours of delivery.[6]

Lincoln, in contrast, was neither sought after to speak at Gettysburg nor universally acclaimed for his performance. The governors had not considered Lincoln for principal speaker because they doubted his suitability "to speak upon such a grave and solemn occasion." With only a limited familiarity with Lincoln as a speaker, the governors had "a fear that the president might lack the requisite sensitivity, or worse, might seize upon the occasion to make a political speech."[7]

Ultimately deciding an invitation was due the president, on November 2—six weeks after Everett had been invited and only two weeks before the dedication—Lincoln was invited to make a few "appropriate" remarks.[8]

So, with the program set, the ceremonies proceeded as charted by the governors. In a single sentence in his diary, John Hay, one of Lincoln's secretaries, summed up the day: "Mr. Stockton made a prayer which thought it was an oration—and Mr. Everett spoke as he always does perfectly—and the President in a firm free way, with more grace than is his wont said his half dozen lines of consecration and the music wailed and we went home through crowded and cheering streets."[9]

The Essence of Being Quotable

Our challenge in defining techniques and strategies professionals can use to merit attention as promotable individuals requires not only understanding why Lincoln's speech, though a secondary consideration to the governors, remains more memorable and enduring than Everett's, but also understanding why, at that time, Everett's speech was preferred by the governors and so enthusiastically acknowledged by the public and the press.

Clearly, few people are capable of speaking or writing with the polish exhibited in Lincoln's 272 words at Gettysburg; nor are most people capable of—nor inclined to—offering a two-hour oration. Yet, there is much to be learned from both the speakers that afternoon of November 19, 1863, about fashioning presentations—both written and oral.

Unlike the phrases readily recalled from Lincoln's speech, in business, being quotable entails establishing a presence as an authority whose thoughts, ideas, interpretations, and conclusions are readily accepted and promoted among colleagues and management. It is a result of having a complete command of the line of thought, complemented by its artful and effective presentation.

One way of thinking about the definition of being quotable in business is the ability to articulate an idea in a manner that people will want to repeat it. It is a style which in professional communication entails "writing that works quietly in the background without calling attention to itself."[10]

A corollary to the previous chapter's discussion regarding how to make the management's job easier, in business crafting an expression of thought that bears repeating constitutes fulfillment of the most basic principle of how to get ahead: Make the boss look good! The ancillary credit management and colleagues gain from employing and sharing your thoughts, arguments, and expressions is, in fact, the source of the direct acknowledgment and credit you will receive.

That is why to understand the means by which to become quotable, we need to examine the synthesis of the six critical agents that made the appearances at Gettysburg notable:

Purpose—demonstrating consistent attention to the intent of the presentation;

Design—providing a clear, discernable flow and arrangement of thought;

Construction—providing a sophistication of grammar and mechanics that produces a harmony of ideas;

Language—establishing cadences and emphases that strike a visceral chord;

Audience Alignment—designing the communication to match the audience's expectations;

Pace—Presenting information at a rate that promotes comprehension and audience comfort.

With the exception of examining purpose, which was addressed in detail in Chapter 2, we'll review each of these factors. In so doing. we will enlist the assistance not only of Lincoln's performance but also make reference to two of the other best-known American speeches: Martin Luther King Jr.'s "I Have a Dream" speech and President Kennedy's Inaugural address.

Design

Audiences recognize patterns. In the cases of both Lincoln and Everett, their speeches followed the time-honored format of funeral orations. By allusion to Athens in the first sentence following his opening comments, Everett signaled his intent to follow an organizational pattern dating back to Pericles and the Peloponnesian Wars: "It was appointed by law in Athens, that the obsequies of the citizens who fell in battle should be performed at the public expense, and in the most honorable manner."[11]

Although less explicit, Lincoln also employs the accepted structure of formal funeral orations: Acknowledging those who paved the path ("Four score"); praising the values and ideals they instilled ("a nation conceived in liberty"); giving context to the oration ("we cannot hallow this ground"); exhorting those in attendance to take up the mantle of the fallen ("It is for us … to be dedicated to the great task remaining"); and concluding with a statement of the magnitude of the debt owed by those who remain ("The world will little note, nor long remember what we say here, but it can never forget what they did here").[12]

Another more common means of providing a design is through themes, sometimes employing a single theme, sometimes two or more interwoven themes. As example, Figure 3.1 depicts two of the principal themes in the "I Have a Dream" speech, one theme time related, the other fulfillment of a promise.

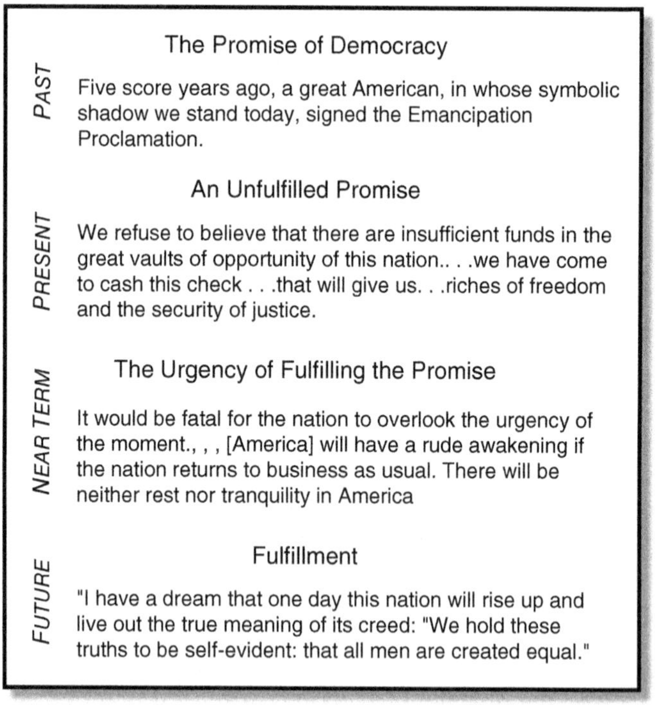

The Promise of Democracy

PAST Five score years ago, a great American, in whose symbolic shadow we stand today, signed the Emancipation Proclamation.

An Unfulfilled Promise

PRESENT We refuse to believe that there are insufficient funds in the great vaults of opportunity of this nation.. . .we have come to cash this check . . .that will give us. . .riches of freedom and the security of justice.

The Urgency of Fulfilling the Promise

NEAR TERM It would be fatal for the nation to overlook the urgency of the moment., , , [America] will have a rude awakening if the nation returns to business as usual. There will be neither rest nor tranquility in America

Fulfillment

FUTURE "I have a dream that one day this nation will rise up and live out the true meaning of its creed: "We hold these truths to be self-evident: that all men are created equal."

Figure 3.1 Depiction of Thematic Design.

Providing a familiar framework accomplishes several objectives that help translate a fleeting presentation into a quotable communication: (1) it allows the audience easily to follow along with the progression of thought; (2) at any point, it gives the audience a sense of how far along you are in the presentation; (3) the comfort with design enhances attention, minimizes distraction; and, perhaps most importantly (4) owing to the ability to follow along with the presentation, increases likelihood critical ideas and noteworthy expressions will be remembered, repeated, and credited to you.

Construction

As noted in the Introduction, from the 19th century forward, grammatical precision has remained a focal point for communication training. However, beyond a narrow focus that promotes precision as exclusively a function of maintaining mechanical correctness, precision in artfully determining word choice and basic structuring of information presentation constitutes a foundation from which to develop sophisticated, dynamic, and quotable communications.

In particular, two often overlooked simple techniques can make profound impacts on the sound and flow of information: (1) selecting and varying sentence openings to amplify audience interest and create a rhythmic path between paragraphs (Table 3.1) and (2) the purposeful utilization and varying use of punctuation to align internal structures, promote emphasis, and maximize comprehension (Table 3.2).

From sentence openers and punctuation, the next impactful element contributing to style and comprehension is the paragraph, "the building blocks with which technical communications are built."[13] In contrast to arguments for conciseness that mistakenly suggest comprehension is a function of factors like sentence and paragraph lengths to be assessed by counting words and reading ease scores, arbitrarily seeking brevity does not aid comprehension, internal cohesion within the paragraph, or the precision of thought.

The real issues in promoting comprehension and precision at the paragraph level lie with guarding against four common, comprehension-limiting errors:

1 Embedding—hiding the main thought,
2 Internal shifting—failing to fulfill announced or implicit expectations,
3 Nonparallel structuring—failing to retain grammatical consistency, and
4 Information confusion—mishandling incorporation of source material (Table 3.3).

Table 3.1 A Range of Sentence Openers

Opener	Explanation	Example
Absolute word/phrase	A parenthetical word or phrase that qualifies the clause or sentence	True, Everett was a better-known speaker than Lincoln and the more likely candidate by the governors.
Adjective clause	A clause functioning as an adjective	Being positioned as we are to evaluate the orations, we can recognize the salient characteristics.
Adverb	A word modifying a verb, adjective, or another adverb	Very clearly, Everett's oration was preferred by the press over that of Lincoln.
Adverb phrase or clause	A phrase or a clause that functions as an adverb	Although Everett spoke longer, he did not necessarily speak more eloquently.
Appositive phrase	A phrase equivalent to a noun is placed near that noun to help identify or explain it	A leader in the movement to save the Union, Everett was the likely choice for vice president on the Constitutional-Union ticket.
Gerundial phrase	A phrase, that by employing a verb with an "ing" ending, functions as a noun	Articulating a position welcomed by the North, Everett's party received a sizeable portion of the popular vote.
Infinitive phrase	A phrase, that by employing a verb in its "to be" form, functions as a noun	To be certain the structure would be recognized, Everett began with an allusion to ancient Athens.
Interjection	A short exclamation	How outstanding, the simple eloquence of a mere 272 words.
Noun clause	A subordinate clause used as a noun	Whichever speaker one prefers, both gentlemen present lessons for us all.
Prepositional phrase	A phrase introduced by a preposition	By the time he rose to speak, Everett had completed extensive research regarding the Greek funeral traditions.

Table 3.2 Practical, Persuasive Punctuation

Pattern	Punctuation	Example
Amplification + punctuation + independent clause	Comma	Speaking first, Everett held the crowd in awed silence.
	Semicolon	He was forceful; Everett artfully laid out the historical argument for preserving the union.
	"Em" Dash	Well known—Everett was the voice of a major political figure who advocated sustaining the union.
	Colon	The Address was well received: It was reprinted verbatim in numerous newspapers.
Independent clause + punctuation + amplification	Multiple options available	Everett had unparalleled credentials, having been Secretary of State, Senator, and Vice-Presidential candidate.
Subject + punctuation + amplification + predicate	Paired Commas	Lincoln, being new to the audiences, faced unique challenges.
	Paired "Em" Dashes	Lincoln—not given to lengthy speeches—was up and down before his photograph could be taken.
	Paired Parentheses	Lincoln (endorsed by Horace Greeley) gained the support of the New York Tribune and the New York Republican establishment.

Table 3.3 Issues with Paragraph Unity and Coherence

Error	Example Sentence	The Issue
Embedding	It is my opinion that a primary reason the press was overly inclined to Everett, a great statesman, was not length, depth, or insights or the occasion of his funeral oration.	The point is not clear: Is the main point focusing on the press, on Everett, his credentials, the occasion, or the oration?
Internal Shifting	The research points to the fact that eighty-five percent of certain newspapers that favored Everett had an inherent bias against Lincoln.	The expectation of clarifying the research instead fails to explain the sampling (exclusively Democrat-leaning newspapers) or the bias (the Republican platform, not Lincoln's speech).
Nonparallel Structuring	The Democrats had little of interest in common with the entire Republican party, the Whig's candidates, the finer points raised by the Constitutionalists—not to mention the Do-Nothing Party.	Lacking parallelism, it is unclear whether the Democrats had opinions about or interests in the Do-Nothing Party as a whole, its candidates, or its platform.
Information Confusion	Pennsylvania voters, 64% who voted for Lincoln, included only half of Alleghany County, the percentages dipping below the totals received by 1856 candidates but not rivaling those voting for Lincoln in 1864.	The statistics and associated information are fragmented and incomplete—depriving statistics of any value or relevance.

By far, one of the most effective means of guarding against such adverse impacts to comprehension is to follow a simple rule promulgated by Dr. Robert R. Rathbone, the founder of MIT's Technical Communication Program: "Put the Whole Before the Parts."[14] Using the first sentence of each paragraph to direct traffic sends a clear message about the paragraph's theme, establishes the paragraph's borders, and provides guideposts that readily distinguish if any of the four comprehension issues just cited exist.

Language

At the heart of communication style is the ability to "turn a phrase." Creating quotable material—as is characteristic of the speeches and writing of Lincoln, Kennedy, and King—involves ability to establish clearly delineated points of emphasis and to offer expressions using cadences that create visceral impressions and enhance recall.

Known as a man who "habitually read things out loud to see how they sounded and ... to hear all-important intonations and rhythms," Lincoln crafted language with the explicit intent of eliciting both an intellectual and a visceral response.[15] A college student who stood "perhaps thirty feet in front of the stand" offered this personal, eyewitness account of the impact of Lincoln's speech at Gettysburg:

> *His simple power and pathos at once held me ... . [The address's] ... clear-cut sentences, its strong monosyllables, were notable. And then the beauty of it! The elevation of thought ... uttered with a rhythmical flow of words that left a musical cadence on the ear.*[16]

For King, the ability to create emphasis through crescendos of images and recognized cadences derived from extensive study of the Bible: His sounds and the visceral reactions invoked a reflection of years standing at the church pulpit.

Kennedy similarly wrote for effect. Theodore Sorenson, who served as a key White House advisor and speechwriter for Kennedy, offered these insights:

> *The test of a text was not how it appeared to the eye, but how it sounded to the ear. His best paragraphs, when read aloud, often had a cadence not unlike blank verse ... . He was fond of alliterative sentences, not solely for reasons of rhetoric but to reinforce the audience's recollection of his reasoning.*

Further explaining Kennedy's purposeful synthesis of sound and reasoning, Sorenson goes on to explain, "his emphasis on a course of reason—rejecting the extremes of either side—helped produce the parallel construction and use of contrasts with which he later became identified."[17]

Of critical importance to all professionals is the knowledge that the voices these men developed were a consequence of consciously and purposely adopted cadences and expressions that appealed to them. In so doing, it is unlikely they were aware that they were employing rhetorical and stylistic devices that have been known and practiced for centuries. What they did know—and the characteristic they shared—was the appreciation that making the presentation easy on the ear translated into ideas that captured attention and expressions that were understood, long remembered, and enthusiastically repeated.

In that regard, every professional has available to them the same tools and techniques that gave power to the works of Lincoln, Kennedy, and King. The challenge is choosing which devices you are most comfortable with, which sound most natural to you, and which come most readily to mind when drafting communications.

There is a vast selection of devices from which to choose—ranging from the basic metaphor and simile we all practiced in high school English classes to devices that, although creating memorable phrases, require highly complicated linguistic constructions.

For example, one of Kennedy's most oft-quoted lines—"Ask not what your country can do for you; ask what you can do for your country"—employs a device known as "antimetabole." A device somewhat impractical in most business contexts, antimetaboles are expressions in which the beginning section and the concluding section of one clause have their positions reversed in the following clause. Although very clever, the device tends to call too much attention to itself and therefore—particularly in a business environment—may be perceived as more contrived than creative.

Rather, as an initial set of practicable stylistic devices, it might be beneficial to consider the suite of devices our three orators had in common (Table 3.4).

Audience Alignment

Unlike the three factors just discussed, respecting audience expectations and audience capacity is not a function of the content of the communication as much as it is a function of the context of the communication.

A reader's or an audience's expectations regarding the communication can focus on a range of factors—the form the communication takes, the language by which it is expressed, the topic being discussed, and, even, the personality or appearance of the speaker. Fulfilling the audience's expectations is in large measure the reason why Everett received a greater acknowledgment at Gettysburg than did Lincoln.

The people gathered at the cemetery knew what to expect when Everett stood to speak. They expected an oration in the accepted traditions of funerals for fallen warriors. They expected, based on his well-known speeches, that he would address himself to maintaining the solvency of the union. And, as was the hallmark of his orations and eulogies for the fallen, the audience expected the poetic diction and vivid language to last for at least an hour or two.

On the other hand, Lincoln, as we noted earlier, was not yet widely known as an orator. Prior to Gettysburg, his acclaim as a speaker was largely confined to the seven Illinois counties where, five years earlier in a losing senatorial campaign, he debated the issue of slavery with Stephen Douglas. Although a significant set of speeches, the localized attention generated by the Lincoln-Douglas debates did not rival Everett's decades of speeches and public service.

Expecting a great oration on the style, length, and substance of the kind presented by Everett, the audience at Gettysburg was not prepared for

Table 3.4 A Practical Selection of Stylistic Devices

Device Name	Explanation	Lincoln	Kennedy	King
ALLITERATION	Recurrence of initial consonant sounds	dead we give increased devotion	dark powers of destruction	in whose symbolic shadow we stand
ALLUSION	Indirect reference to a famous person or event	Four score and seven years (Declaration)	to that world assembly of sovereign states (United Nations)	1963 is not an end but a beginning ("Kennedy's Inaugural Address")
ANADIPLOSIS	Repeating the concluding words in successive sections	that that nation or any nation	been committed, and to which we are committed.	come to cash a check, a check
ANAPHORA	Repeating the same beginning words	We are engaged ... we are met .... We have come	let both sides ... let both sides	one hundred years later ... one hundred years later
ANTITHESIS	Juxtaposing ideas to emphasize the contrast between them	The brave men living and dead	We celebrate today not a victory of party but a celebration of freedom	joyous daybreak to end the long night of captivity
ASSONANCE	Repeating similar vowel sounds	Our father brought forth	jungle of suspicion	On the high plane of dignity and discipline
ASYNDETON	Omitting conjunctions within a series	Government of the people, by the people, and for the people	pay any price, bear any burden, meet any hard-ship, hardship	every valley ... every hill ... every mountain ...
CLIMAX	Arranging items in a series of increasing emphasis	Government of the people, by the people, and for the people	born in this century ... unwilling to witness	free at last, free at last, thank God Almighty, we're free at last
EPANALEPSIS	Repeating the same words or clause at both the beginning and end	We take increased devotion to that cause for which they gave the last full measure of devotion	Let us explore what problems unite us instead ... hose problems that divide us	It is a dream deeply rooted in the American dream

(Continued)

Table 3.4 (Continued)

Device Name	Explanation	Lincoln	Kennedy	King
EPISTROPHE	Repeating the same ending word	Whether that nation, or any nation	the power to destroy nations under ... control of all nations	a person ... cannot vote ... has nothing for which to vote
LITOTE	Understating by using an unusual equivalent for the expected term	Shall not perish	we cannot become the prey of hostile powers	I am not unmindful that
METONYMY	Substituting a closely associated feature for the item being cited	A new birth of freedom (conclusion of the war and slavery)	huts and villages (third-world countries)	interposition and nullification (segregation)
PARALLELISM	Arranging items using the same syntactical construction	Now we are engaged ... we are met ... we have come	united ... divided	to work together, to pray together, to struggle together, to
PERSONIFICATION	Providing an inanimate object with human or animal characteristics	the world will little note ...	this hemisphere intends to remain the master of its own house	justice rolls down like waters... righteousness like a mighty stream
POLYSYNDETON	The opposite of asyndeton, inserting conjunctions within a series	—	where the strong are just and the weak secure, and the peace preserve	and the crooked places will be made straight, and the glory ... and all flesh
RHETORICAL QUESTION	Phrasing an idea as a question whose answer is evident	—	Can we forge ... ... will you join me ... ?	when will you be satisfied?
TRICOLON	Presenting three syntactically equivalent phrases, clauses, or sentences	We cannot dedicate, we cannot consecrate, we cannot hallow	both sides over-burdened, both rightly alarmed, yet both racing	Some of you have come from ... Some of you have come ... Some of you have come

Lincoln's few "appropriate" remarks. His presentation—not a traditional eulogy, not a speech delivered with great flourish, nor one that lasted more than a few minutes—did not rise to the level of the attendees' expectations (even if it was consistent with the request of the governors who had invited Lincoln).

Indicative of much of the press's response, the *Indiana State Sentinel* offered a scathing review of Lincoln's performance: "The cheek of every American must tingle with shame as he reads the silly, flat, and dishwatery utterances of the man who has to be pointed out to intelligent foreigners as the president of the United States."[18]

Similar disappointment was voiced regarding the speech's brevity. Clark E. Carr, a delegate to the Cemetery Commission from Lincoln's home state of Illinois, recorded this response to the speech:

So short a time that Mr. Lincoln was before them that the people could scarcely believe their eyes ... They could not possibly, in so short a time, mentally grasp the ideas that were conveyed, nor even their substance. Time and again expressions of disappointment were made to me. Many persons said to me that they would have supposed that on such a great occasion the President would have made a speech.[19]

The point here, although simple, is vitally important: When planning a communication, carefully consider what the audience is likely expecting. For an assignment to be thoroughly complete, it must be substantive, artful, and consistent with the expectations: What people expect to see, in the format they expect to see it, and delivered at a pace that allows for ease of comprehension. If the audience gets distracted by the needed effort to try to understand why there appear to be significant disconnects between expectations for the presentation and its delivery, the opportunity to make a positive impression is lost.

Pace

This last factor, pace at which information is presented, becomes particularly important when dealing with material that is unfamiliar to the audience, highly complex, or that demands a high level of specificity. Presenting information at an inappropriately slow pace suggests a disregard for the audience's time and intellect. A pace that is too fast, by contrast, discourages attention by tacitly demanding the audience work too hard to follow the train of thought; eventually no longer able to keep up, the audience just drifts away. In either case—too slow or too fast—an error in pace lessens the likelihood of making management's job easy or making management look good.

As with many of the tools and techniques we have been examining, fixing or avoiding a problem with pace is straightforward: Speed of information delivery is principally linked to the amount of repetition and elaboration. Therefore, with a fairly homogeneous audience, the pace can be readily targeted at the known level of familiarity with the subject.

When dealing with a diverse audience with significantly varying degrees of familiarity with the subject matter, the most prudent course is to envision a subset of the attendees that could be reasonably assumed to have a modest level of knowledge—neither experts nor totally uninformed. Introducing repetition and elaboration targeted at that middle ground will accommodate individuals who need more time and assistance to follow along, while, at the same time, being fast enough so as to maintain the engagement of others who come with better knowledge.

For instance, considering our copier management presentation, a suitable target might be to tailor the pace of information to the Director of the Safety Department. That department can be assumed to be less reliant on comprehensive copier services than say the Research Department (which requires high capacity and a range of standard and non-standard functions), but more reliant on services than, say, General Counsel (with minimal copier support needs).

Developing Your Style

The cumulative power of artfully applying the tools and techniques to project a sophisticated communication style is perhaps best summarized in two quotations: In a section of an 1897 unpublished paper, Winston Churchill, one of England's most accomplished statesmen and orators, addressed how the "Scaffolding of Rhetoric" contributes to the ultimate "accumulation of argument":

> *The climax of oratory is reached by a rapid succession of waves of sound and vivid pictures. The audience is delighted by the changing scenes presented to their imagination. Their ear is tickled by the rhythm of the language. The enthusiasm rises. A series of facts is brought forward all pointing in a common direction. The end appears in view before it is reached. The crowd anticipates the conclusion and the last words fall amid a thunder of assent.*[20]

Expanding on Churchill's point regarding the visceral impact of an effective communication style, just three years after the end of WW II,

J. Robert Oppenheimer—the father of the atomic bomb—offered this perception of style's direct impact on all aspects of contemporary life:

> *The problem of doing justice to the implicit, the imponderable, and the unknown is of course not unique to politics. It is always with us in science, it is with us in the most trivia of personal affairs, and it is one of the great problems of writing and of all forms of art The means by which it is solved is sometimes called style. It is style which complements affirmation with humility; it is style that makes it possible to act effectively, but not absolutely; it is style that enables us to find harmony between the pursuit of ends essential to us, and the regard for the views, the sensibilities, the aspirations of those to whom the problem may appear in another light; it is style which is the deference that action pays to certainty; it is above all style through which power defers to reason.*[21]

As we have noted, and as H.L. Mencken, one of the most influential literary critics of the early 20th century, asserted: "Any human being who can speak English understandably has all the materials necessary to write English clearly, and even beautifully … . If a man can think in English at all, he can find words enough to express his ideas."[22] That truth was borne out by Lincoln, Kennedy, and King. The two things they shared were a command of the English language and a goal of making their speeches and writing artful and memorable.

Both these elements are available to every professional; the difference of who masters the art and who doesn't is a matter of desire—not talent. In that regard, creating your own style begins with two concurrent efforts. The first action is making the decision to take advantage of the tools and devices we have been discussing. This can be accomplished by taking a moment to consider tools, techniques, or devices every time you sit down to begin drafting a communication or presentation: For instance, asking yourself.

Would a certain sentence opener set the right tone or signal?

Could a specific point be made more powerful by employing antithesis?

Could an effective cadence amplify a concluding point by presenting it as a tricolon?

Actively questioning your choices of expression, beginning to listen for sounds and rhythms you find pleasing, slowly but surely will begin to shape your personal style. Every word and phrasing choice and every device employed—over time—solidifies into a recognizable and individually personalized representation of you, your thinking, and your personality.

Complementing the use of the techniques and tools is the capability enhanced through active listening. Whether reading or attending a presentation, listen to the sounds words make. Unlike our contemporary educational model, the 17th, 18th, and 19th centuries inculcated elements of style by having students copy out in long hand page after page from essays and speeches, all the while assimilating stylistic elements as they worked.

Whether copying works of the masters or studying the voices that you find most compelling, developing a style is a matter of identifying the sounds words make on paper, of listening to the communications you author to assess more than just the substance or the frame of the argument. Developing a style is achieved through practice and study: What is practiced becomes routine; what becomes routine, becomes one's style.

Notes

1 Revised Report Made to the Legislature of Pennsylvania, Soldiers National Cemetery, at Gettysburg (Harrisburg, P.A.: Singerly and Myers, 1867).
2 Edward Everett, *The Great Issues Now Before Our Country, an Oration* (New York: James G. Gregory, 1861).
3 Svend Petersen, *The Gettysburg Addresses: The Story of Two Orations* (New York: Frederick Ungar Publishing Company, 1963).
4 Edward Everett, *Address at the Consecration of the National Cemetery at Gettysburg* (Boston: Little, Brown & Company, 1864), 29.
5 Ted Widmer, "The Other Gettysburg Address," *New York Times*, November 19, 2013, https://archive.nytimes.com/opinionator.blogs.nytimes.com/2013/11/19/the-other-gettysburg-address.
6 "The Dedication of the Gettysburg Cemetery—The Vindication of Maj. Gen. Curtis—The Speakership—Iowans from Libby Prison," *Muscatine Weekly Journal*, December 4, 1863. Vol. 15, No. 20, 4, https://chroniclingamerica.loc.gov/lccn/sn84027253/1863-12-04/ed-1/seq-1/#date1=1863&index=16&rows=20&words=Cemetery+Gettysburg&searchType=basic&sequence=0&state=&date2=1864&proxtext=cemetery+Gettysburg&y=0&x=0&dateFilterType=yearRange&page=4.
7 Douglas L. Wilson, *Lincoln's Sword* (New York: Alfred A, Knopf, 2006).
8 Julius B. Remensnyder, "Personal Memories of Lincoln: President Lincoln's Address at Gettysburg," *Outlook*, February 13, 1918, 243.
9 Remensynder, "Personal Memories."
10 Robert R. Rathbone, *Communicating Technical Information* (Addison Wesley: Reading, MA, 1972).
11 Everett, *Address at the Consecration*, 29.
12 Garry Wills, *Lincoln at Gettysburg: The Words That Remade America* (New York: Simon and Schuster, 1992).
13 Robert Rathbone, *Communicating Technical Information*.
14 Robert Rathbone, *Communicating Technical Information*.
15 Wilson, *Lincoln's Sword*.
16 Remensynder, "Personal Memories," 244.

17 Theodore C. Sorenson, *Kennedy* (New York: Harper & Row: New York, 1965).
18 "Special Correspondence from the Chicago Times," *Indiana State Sentinel*, November 30, 1863,8. https://chroniclingamerica.loc.gov/lccn/sn82014306/1863-11-30/ed-1/seq-2/#date1=1863&index=0&rows=20&words=cemetery+Gettysburg&searchType=basic&sequence=0&state=&date2=1864&proxtext=cemetery+Gettysburg&y=0&x=0&dateFilterType=yearRange&page=8.
19 Wilson, *Lincoln's Sword*.
20 Winston Churchill, "The Scaffolding of Rhetoric," November 1897, https://winstonchurchill.org/wp-content/uploads/2016/06/THE_SCAFFOLDING_OF_RHETORIC.pdf.
21 J. Robert Oppenheimer, "The Open Mind," in *The Open Mind* (New York: Simon and Schuster, 1955), 54.
22 H.L. Mencken, "On Style," in *A Mencken Chrestomathy* (New York: Alfred A. Knopf, 1974).

Chapter 4

Speaking Graphically

A commercial nuclear reactor's function is straightforward: Heat water to produce steam and use that steam to drive a turbine which, in turn, powers a generator, creating electricity. Complexity, however, arises with producing and controlling the heat. Uranium oxide, compacted into small pellets, is encased in long, thin rods. Passing through the rods, neutrons collide with and split encased uranium atoms. This "fissioning" releases energy, principally in the form of heat. At the same time, it releases neutrons, resulting in a "chain" reaction as an ever-expanding series of neutrons replicates the process.

Controlling the chain reaction (and thereby the heat and power) is accomplished by varying the positions of control rods, rods interspersed among the fuel rods containing strong neutron absorbers such as cadmium. Beyond regulating control rods manually, in an emergency, control rods drop immediately into the core, instantaneously terminating fission activity.

However, in one instance, not all designed elements—human or mechanical—worked as planned. Like all commercial reactors, the pair of Three Mile Island (TMI) reactors just outside Harrisburg, Pennsylvania, was complex. TMI-2 housed approximately 100 tons of uranium contained in 36,816 fuel rods—208 in each of 177 fuel assemblies. In addition, assemblies each held 69 control rods and 52 instrument tubes monitoring an array of operating parameters.

On Wednesday, March 28, 1979, at precisely 36 seconds after 4:00 a.m., pumps that supply cooling water to the reactor vessel stopped—depriving the vessel of coolant needed to maintain temperatures. Loss of coolant triggered a series of inter-related actions, which, as designed, occurred within seconds: The turbine was shut down to reduce mounting pressure within the cooling water holding tank due to its constricted flow; the valve atop that tank opened, releasing steam and water onto the containment building floor; and then the reactor shut down.

DOI: 10.4324/9781003455585-5

Also, as designed, three emergency coolant pumps immediately activated to preclude one of the most serious reactor accident scenarios: A-loss-of-coolant accident (LOCA) in which the unregulated heat generated by ongoing fission jeopardizes the integrity of fuel rods and the containment vessel, while also posing a potential for explosions due to hydrogen buildup.

Unfortunately, although confirming the pumps' activation, the control room operator overlooked two indicators signaling that the feed line from the pumps was sealed: No coolant was reaching the reactor core. Exacerbating conditions, a second indicator was misread: Whereas operators reasonably assumed an unlit indicator meant the valve on the coolant holding tank had closed, terminating further steam and water release, the unlighted position, in fact, signified the valve remained in the open position.

Consequently, open for more than two hours, the valve allowed more than 32,000 gallons to accumulate on the containment room floor. During that time, deprived of coolant, the heat in the reactor vessel intensified. At its highest level, temperatures reached 4300 °F, a few hundred degrees shy of melting the fuel rods.

The entire event, as the Presidential Commission investigating the accident concluded, needn't have happened: "Had the … control room operators [simply] closed a backup valve … the accident at Three Mile Island would have remained little more than a minor inconvenience."[1] Instead, that evening on the CBS News, Walter Cronkite painted an image that continues to overshadow the nuclear industry:

> It was the first step in a nuclear nightmare … . probably the worst reactor accident to date. There was no serious contamination of workers. But a nuclear safety group said that radiation inside the plant is eight times the deadly level, so strong that after passing through a three-foot thick concrete wall, it can be measured a mile away.[2]

So, what caused the accident at TMI-2? "At the time, bureaucratic poobahs blamed the near miss on a favorite scapegoat … . Operator Error. But the fact is, TMI wasn't a user error; the people operating the reactor never had a chance. TMI was a failure of design."[3] That "failure" was, in large measure, a design that allowed a misleading and ineffective presentation of graphical and statistical information to determine operator actions and decisions.

"To a casual visitor, [a] control room can be an intimidating place, with messages coming from the loudspeaker of the plant's paging system; panel upon panel of red, green, amber, and white lights; and alarms that sound or flash warnings many times each hour."[4] In the emergency unfurling the morning of March 28, 1978, the "seriously insufficient" and magnified flashing of information transformed the control room into an "intimidating place" for experienced control room operators.[5]

Spread across 900 sq. ft of display panels, more than 100 of the 1,900 annunciators (indicators using sounds and lights) began to alarm. Yet the sheer number of active alarms did not in-and-of-itself explain why confusion persisted. That morning the control room design failed to meet basic design expectations needed to safely operate: "The single most critical design requirement ... is the effective display of information ... information must be easily seen and read, well organized, and unambiguous in its content and meaning."[6]

Even limiting discussion to issues of information design most immediately relevant to the broader business world makes evident the breadth of challenges experienced by the operators:

- Inconsistent information—Indicators lacked consistent labeling requiring operator judgments about how to interpret display information.
- Poorly organized information—Relative positioning of indicators did not follow a reasoned organizational logic, making it hard to integrate vital information.
- Invalid information—Unconventional presentations (e.g., using an unlit indicator to indicate an active valve) resulted in misinterpretations of data.
- Nonavailability of information—Information essential to decision-making was unavailable (e.g., there was no indicator associated with holding tank coolant flow).
- Information overload—There was no means to differentiate critical from less significant alarms or their sequencing when large numbers of alarms sounded simultaneously.
- Procedure inadequacy—Supplemental written response instructions were incomplete.
- Inaccurate prioritization of information—Noncritical displays (e.g., minor electrical systems) were disproportionately large and given inappropriate prominent placement.

Summarizing the consequences of poorly designed visualization of information, the Commission assessing the accident at TMI came to the following conclusion:

> At TMI, *because the operators had to base their decisions on a situation which was not clear, many of the actions they took to influence the process during the accident significantly exacerbated the consequences of the initiating events. [Operators] were unable to satisfactorily process the large amounts of data available to them and had difficulty distinguishing between significant and insignificant information.*[7]

Purposeful Depiction: Three Models

The root of the problem at TMI was not so much that the display of information didn't perform as planned; the problem was that the presentation design was not planned with sufficient consideration of the training received by those individuals who would use the information, precisely what information they would need, and the conditions under which the information would be applied.

Rather, control room designers assumed information would be used exclusively during normal, routine operations at the plant. They were convinced under off-normal situations, the reactor's automated and redundant safety systems would take over, a commonly endorsed strategy within the nuclear industry known as "defense-in-depth." Not fully anticipating the operators' dependence on the display in diagnosing and resolving emergency conditions, designers assumed sufficient information—were it ever needed by the operators—could be found within the universe of annunciators and procedures.

As exhibited in the TMI-2 example, the cleverness of the design reflected the sophisticated ability many professionals have with manipulating graphics software and the ability they have in generating colorful and elaborate graphical and statistical displays. What it also shows is that developing more effective visualization is not a matter of offering a primer on the mechanics of creating displays. Rather, enhancing display of graphical and statistical information in business is a function of developing the skills to critically assess the adequacy and effectiveness of the presented material. It is recognition the visualization of information is successful only when the display has both a precisely defined purpose and a purposeful depiction that delivers that purpose—when both the "why" of the presentation and the "how" of the presentation align to send a clear, unmistakable, and powerful message.

Even the most creative and elaborate presentation will miss the mark if the depiction—the design of the graphic—is mistaken as the measure of success. Accordingly, what professionals need is practical guidance on how to critically assess both the adequacy and effectiveness of presentation. It requires an understanding that successfully communicating with graphical and statistical displays is a function of the complementary relationship between purpose and depiction. It requires—as concisely described in the Nuclear Regulatory Commission guidance for control room design cited earlier—providing visual presentations that are "easily seen and read, well organized, and unambiguous in its content and meaning."

So as to concentrate discussion on the means of assessing graphical and statistical displays rather than on the mechanics of their creation, we are going to derive the critical attributes of successful visualization through in-depth examination of the work of three individuals, who, in the 19th century, helped define and establish the concepts of visually presenting information.

These three people—who predated development of computers, were unassisted by sophisticated drawing aids, and were devoid of extensive libraries of graphic design—profoundly impacted the art and technique of visualizing information. Their works selected here are also illustrative of the three most common situations in professional communication in which visualization of information is most applicable: Depicting What Has Happened; Depicting Why Something Has Happened; and Making a Case for What Needs to Be Done.

Depicting What Has Happened

In the mid-19th century, Charles Joseph Minard, a French civil engineer, recognized that industrial enterprise was increasingly dependent on data and statistics. As he understood it, "The growth of statistical research in our times has made felt the need to record the results in forms less dry, more useful, and able to be explored more rapidly than numbers alone."[8]

In defining a means to "free statistics from the kind of scorn where it remained for a long time," Minard advanced visualization techniques from simple bar graphs (referred to by him as "graphic tables") to "figurative maps"—flow diagrams illustrating the "traffic" of people, merchandise, and supplies.[9]

These portrayals succeeded, as celebrated by one of his contemporaries, by replacing "complicated columns of statistical data" with "mathematically proportioned" images, that "manifest immediately the natural consequences or the comparisons unforeseen."[10]

Although having authored more than 40 figurative maps in support of commercial applications, Minard's contributions to the discipline of data visualization rest principally on a single image: A depiction of Napolean's 1812 invasion of Russia.

Acclaimed by Edward Tufte, the leading authority on visualization of data, as perhaps "the best statistical graphic ever drawn," its power and appeal reside in its simplicity of design that interweaves six variables associated with troop size, troop movement, location, and temperatures (Figure 4.1).[11] It is a design, as denoted in Edward Tufte's *Beautiful Evidence*, that satisfies what he contends are the six "principles of analytic design":

- Showing causality,
- Showing comparisons and differences,
- Showing multivariate data,
- Integrating evidence (i.e., aligning text and images),
- Describing the evidence (e.g., identifying sources),
- Contents count.[12]

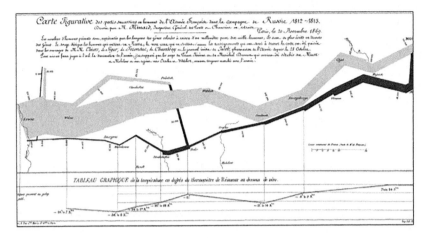

Figure 4.1 Minard's "Russian Campaign".[14]

The first five of the six principles are immediately evident in Minard's graphic. The final principle, however, would not necessarily be considered successful if measured by expectations placed on visualized information in the contemporary business world. In Minard's graphic, we do not have a factually accurate representation of Napoleon Bonaparte's march; rather, as explained by his son-in-law, Minard was intending to portray his "premonition" of the "appalling catastrophes which were going to shatter France" under the current rule of Napoleon III.[13]

Given his assumed purpose helps explain the factors that an accurate and precise visualization of information must seek to avoid:

• A challenging complexity,
• Misleading impressions, and
• Questionable factual accuracy.

Challenging Complexity

In depicting the circumstances of Napoleon's march, the variables are introduced using somewhat conflicting modes of expression, requiring attention and significant mental effort to grasp the breadth of information: A table across the entire bottom indicates temperatures; radial lines link temperatures to troop strength; colored areas differentiate the advance from the retreat; and small type and short wavy lines identify select towns and rivers along the route of the march.

Competing for attention, these interwoven variables, rather than making the intention "immediately manifest," require protracted study. In the end, one is left with an impression rather than a conclusive recognition of purpose. And, upon further study, a question arises as to the impression's validity.

Misleading Impressions

Rather than providing any specific detail or indication about where or when major battles occurred that had significant impact on troop strength, the graphic's design gives an implied prominence to the temperatures along the route. This prominence gives rise to the impression that the principal failure of Napoleon's march resulted from not having anticipated the intensity of the Russian winter. On the contrary, on closer inspection of the area showing the shrinking size of Napoleon's force, it is clear subfreezing temperatures—as indicated by the radial lines—occur during the retreat: The advance toward Moscow takes place in the summer months; winter sets in as Napoleon attempts to escape the Russian winter.

Moreover, as history tells us, the majority of losses incurred by Napoleon's army did not result from intemperate weather or from wounds: Of the more than 300,000 men Napoleon lost, the "majority of those deaths, perhaps 200,000, were from disease, with typhus the lead killer."[15]

Questionable Accuracy

Along with misleading impressions, two particular inaccuracies introduced by Minard contribute to the mistaken conclusion that temperature fueled the catastrophic losses accompanying the march on Moscow: (1) The size of the force is presented as a gradient rather than as distinct values. Generalizing numbers while masking the impacts of several key battles blurs the fact that the numbers are not valid. (2) As the notes Minard added to the graphic explain, "in order to better judge with the eye the diminution of the army," several battalions not part of the central force are added in as part of the calculation of troop size.

Considering these issues pertaining to Minard's graphic along with lessons derived from the assessment of the TMI-2 accident suggests key factors to be considered when assessing the visualization of information (Table 4.1).

Table 4.1 Summary Assessment of Minard's "Russian Campaign"

Napoleon's March

Communicating Purpose		Design Effectiveness	
Information clear	√	Show causality	X (Incorrectly implied)
Information sufficient	X	Show comparisons and differences	√
Information organized	√	Show multivariate data	√
Message clear	X	Completely integrate evidence	√
Message unambiguous	X	Adequately describe evidence	X
Depiction free from distractions	√	Uniqueness	√
Depiction free from misinterpretations	X	Attractiveness	√

Depicting Why It Happened

The opening paragraph of an 1852 British government *Report on the Mortality of Cholera in England, 1848–1849* painted an indelible image of the dire challenge facing the country:

> *If a Foreign Army had landed on the coast of England, seized all the seaports, sent detachments over the surrounding districts, ravaged the population through summer, after harvest destroyed more than a thousand lives a day for several days in succession, and, in the year it held possession of the country, slain fifty-three thousand two hundred and ninety-three men, women, and children—the task of registering the Dead would be inexpressibly painful; and the pain is not greatly diminished by the circumstance that in the calamity to be described, the minister of destruction was a Pestilence.*[16]

As cholera persisted over the course of two decades in England, a range of theories were postulated about its causes and transmission. Most favored among theories was the idea that the spread was caused by "miasma"—"bad air" emitted by rotting organic matter. Yet, as the 1852 report recorded, several competing theories—all without any scientific substantiation—remained popular:

- "The theory of volcanic agency" blamed "poisonous elements generated in subterraneous reservoirs and diffused in the surrounding atmosphere."

- A "deficiency of electricity" was proposed as the primary cause of the epidemic.
- Claiming the virus began "in the temperate zone [and] has been unquestionably most fatal in the hot season of the year," one theory suggested heat to be the cause.
- Lastly, a "deficiency of ozone" necessary to decompose "miasmic matters thrown into the atmosphere" was postulated as the source of the conveyance.

Against this backdrop, the report noted a "simple" and plausible theory proposed by Dr. Snow: "water discharges of the cholera patients may, under the present system of water supply, be distributed unchanged to nearly every house in London, where water is used for drink, ablution, and washing."[17] Yet, although assumed plausible, the theory still lacked irrefutable evidence if it was to dissuade the public and the scientific community from competing theories.

The genesis of that proof came from a news article that not only indicated government statistics suggested "the influence of water supply … could … be detected in the progress of the epidemic," but also set out a methodology that Snow subsequently adopted.

> [To] measure the effect of good or bad water supply it is requisite to find two classes of inhabitants living on the same level, moving in equal space, enjoying an equal share of the means of existence, engaged in the same pursuit but differing in this respect—that one drinks water from Battersea, the other from Kew.[18]

Initiating the first comprehensive epidemiological study of a "very large population," *On the Mode of Communication of Cholera*, Snow conclusively identified the differences between communities wherein one "suffered excessively from cholera … [the other] … suffered but very little." One community was receiving water "containing the sewage of London … [the other] a water-supply quite free from such contamination."[19]

Within a manuscript of some 150 pages, the convincing culminated in the visualization of the argument in a single table and an accompanying graphic. Detailing information on more than a dozen co-located districts, the table provided statistics regarding population sizes, deaths from cholera, deaths by percentages of district populations, and the source of each district's water supply. The graphic, immediately following the table, offered a map of the section of London encompassed by the table, overlaid with colored areas depicting the water suppliers (Figures 4.2 and 4.3).

TABLE VI.

Sub-Districts.	Population in 1851.	Deaths from Cholera in 1853.	Deaths by Cholera in each 100,000 living.	Water Supply.
St. Saviour,Southwark	19,709	45	227	
St. Olave	8,015	19	237	
St. John, Horsleydown	11,360	7	61	
St. James,Bermondsey	18,899	21	111	
St. Mary Magdalen	13,934	27	193	
Leather Market	15,295	23	153	Southwark and
Rotherhithe*	17,805	20	112	Vauxhall Water
Wandsworth	9,611	3	31	Company only.
Battersea	10,560	11	104	
Putney	5,280	—	—	
Camberwell	17,742	9	50	
Peckham	19,444	7	36	
Christchurch,Southwk.	16,022	7	43	
Kent Road	18,126	37	204	
Borough Road	15,862	26	163	
London Road	17,836	9	50	
Trinity, Newington	20,922	11	52	
St. Peter, Walworth	29,861	23	77	
St. Mary, Newington	14,033	5	35	Lambeth Water
Waterloo (1st part)	14,088	1	7	Company, and
Waterloo (2nd part)	18,348	7	38	Southwark and
Lambeth Church (1st part)	18,409	9	48	Vauxhall Company.
Lambeth Church (2nd part)	26,784	11	41	
Kennington (1st part)	24,261	12	49	
Kennington (2nd part)	18,848	6	31	
Brixton	14,610	2	13	
Clapham	16,290	10	61	
St. George,Camberwell	15,849	6	37	
Norwood	3,977	—	—	Lambeth Water
Streatham	9,023	—	—	Company only.
Dulwich	1,632	—	—	
First 12 sub-districts	167,654	192	114	Southwk. & Vaux.
Next 16 sub-districts	301,149	182	60	Both Companies.
Last 3 sub-districts	14,632	—	—	Lambeth Comp.

* A part of Rotherhithe was supplied by the Kent Water Company ; but there was no cholera in this part.

Figure 4.2 Table Correlating Mortality Rates with Water Supply.

The clarity of the argument—its visualization in both statistical and graphical formats—was conclusive, powerful, and persuasive enough to change the course of how cholera came to be contained. As Dr. Snow concluded, and the medical community sanctioned, the data presented in the table and figure was unchallengeable—and became the basis for

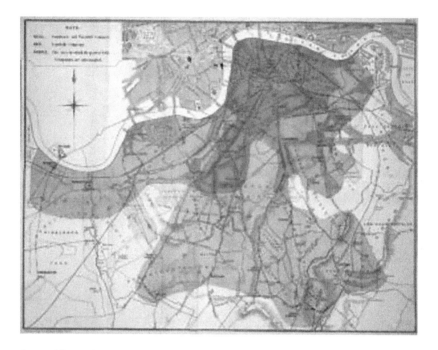

Figure 4.3 Dr. Snow's Map of South London Depicting Water Suppliers.

public hygiene measures forestalling any further serious cholera outbreaks in the city.:

> As there is no difference whatever, either in the houses or the people receiving the supply of the two Water Companies, or in any of the physical conditions with which they are surrounded, it is obvious that no experiment could have been devised which would more thoroughly test the effect of water supply on the progress of cholera than this, which circumstances placed ready made before the observer.[20]

That confidence in the undeniability of the effectiveness of the visualization is readily confirmed using the assessment table we have established (Table 4.2).

Depicting What Needs to Happen

Paralleling Dr. Snow's work, Florence Nightingale provides an example of a graphic underpinning an effort to promote action. Although often

Table 4.2 Summary Assessment of Snow's Graphic on the Transmission of Cholera

Spread of Cholera

Communicating Purpose		Design Effectiveness	
Information clear	√	Show causality	X
Information sufficient	√	Show comparisons and differences	√
Information organized	√	Show multivariate data	√
Message clear	√	Completely integrate evidence	√
Message unambiguous	√	Adequately describe evidence	X
Depiction free from distractions	X	Uniqueness	X
Depiction free from misinterpretations	√	Attractiveness	X

portrayed as the lady with the lamp administering to soldiers on the battlefields of the Crimean War, a trained mathematician, Nightingale contended statistics was "the most important science in the world."[21] Like Dr. Snow, she fought for improved hygiene and curtailing the unchecked transmission of disease; and, like Minard, her focal point was the "loss of an army."[22] However, unlike either of them, her work was neither pure depiction nor proof of a concept, but, rather, an explicit call to action.

Working as the Superintendent of the Hospital for Invalid Gentlewomen when the war began, she was solicited by the Secretary of War to serve as the head of nursing at the military hospitals in Turkey. There she experienced the horrendous conditions wherein mortality rates from illnesses and diseases like typhus and cholera exceeded the rate of deaths resulting from battle: By war's end in 1856, 16,323 of the 21,097 soldiers lost had died due to disease.

Returning to England after the war, Nightingale actively advocated for changes in hygiene and the administration of medical care. And as her statistical studies expanded, so did her sophistication in the art of graphical display of information. In her early works, statistics were commonly displayed using basic bar graphs, but with her 1858 publication, Mortality of the British Army, she introduced a totally new and innovative technique of her own invention for displaying information.

Provided as a foldout at the back of her manuscript, the diagram, which she referred to as a "bat's wing," offered a highly sophisticated—and, what might be considered, an extremely complex—representation of the mortality rate experienced by soldiers in military hospitals. As the text on her graphic elaborates:

The inner circle shows the mortality which the army would have experienced if it had been subject to the same rate which prevailed in one of the unhealthiest cities of England (Manchester).

The distances between the center and the second circle, the second and the third, etc. each represent 100 deaths in 1000 living—the annual rate of mortality in any particular month is shown by the length of the radial line extending from the center in the direction of the month indicated on the outer circle.

Although a striking graphic, the complexity—the amount of effort needed to appreciate the message—limited its impact upon the public and on the British medical community. Accordingly, the following year, Nightingale teamed up with Harriet Martineau, a well-known activist who had published extensively on an array of societal issues including women's rights and abolition of slavery. The collaboration, *England and Her Soldiers*, laid out an argument of similar detail to Nightingale's 1858 treatise but with a decidedly different tone.

Although the book's opening sentence declared "This book is not a work of invention," Martineau's text, assumed an approachable narrative style designed to make the complex subject more accessible and more compelling—a style aptly demonstrated by a single paragraph:

In 1851 ... the effective force of the army was 136,277. If these men had lived as ordinary English people of the same time of life do, they would have lost 1,238 by death. If they lived in the healthiest places, the deaths would have been 1,051. And what was the actual rate of mortality of them, as British soldiers of all arms? Why, 2,381. At that modern date, and in that season of peace, more than twice as many of our soldiers died as if they had remained civilians.[23]

Supporting this approach, Nightingale recast her graphic, presenting the same amount of detail as the original version, but improving the effectiveness of the visualization. Although still complex, the new foldout introduced significant adjustments: Eliminating statistical detail from the 1858 drawing shifted attention to magnitudes of losses rather than distracting viewers by requiring them to make calculations; radial lines were replaced by colored areas. In addition to enhancing visual impact, the design change made the magnitude of losses from disease (as opposed to those caused by wounds and other causes) more pronounced.

To highlight the initial innovation and its subsequent enhancement, Figure 4.4 juxtaposes the 1858 and 1859 graphics.[24] Table 4.3 provides the assessment of the individual attributes of the graphic.

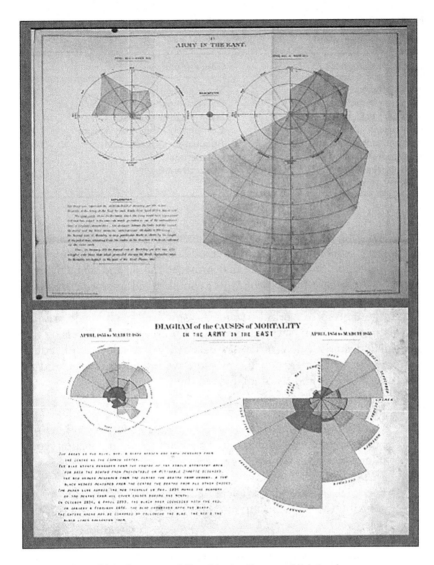

Figure 4.4 Two Most Recognized Graphics by Florence Nightingale.

Proceeding with Purpose

Placing the preceding discussion in perspective, we might now better understand the overarching problem that made responding to the incident at TMI-2 so difficult. Operators single-mindedly pursuing clarification regarding what needed to be done were overwhelmed by information presented with equal

Table 4.3 Summary Assessment of Nightingale's Amy in the East

Mortality in Crimean War

Communicating Purpose		Design Effectiveness	
Information clear	X	Show causality	√
Information sufficient	√	Show comparisons and differences	√
Information organized	√	Show multivariate data	√
Message clear	√	Completely integrate evidence	√
Message unambiguous	√	Adequately describe evidence	X
Depiction free from distractions	X	Uniqueness	√
Depiction free from misinterpretations	√	Attractiveness	√

intensity signaling what specifically was happening, why it was happening, the impending consequences, and actions required. What operators did not have was a presentation of information that provided "clear and unambiguous meaning"—in this case, the steps to ensure a complete and an expedient path to resolution of the impending crisis.

Given the analysis of works by Minard, Snow, and Nightingale, we can define a straightforward, seven-step process for creating and assessing the graphical and statistical information displays we develop—with equal attention to ensuring clarity of the message we intend to convey and to application of the principles of analytic design.

Step 1 Identify Key Ideas
Draft a list of the main points to be made, including ranking the points in terms of how essential they are to communicating your intended message.

Step 2 Define Contributions
For each point, in complete sentences, state how the point contributes to achieving an effective communication of the message.

Step 3 Determine Formats
For each point, identify the format you intend to use (e.g., text, image, spreadsheet, chart, table).

Step 4 Conduct Initial Assessment
Considering the complete set of points to be made, ask the ten questions inspired by our examination of the works of Minard, Snow, and Nightingale:

• What specifically is my intended message and the reaction I want to solicit?

- Will the information provided make my point or assertion as clear as possible?
- How much information needs to be displayed (including text, labeling, legends)?
- Is all the information essential?
- Are all the variables essential and sufficiently inter-related to avoid distracting from one another or from the message as a whole?
- Is the information sufficiently complex to warrant dividing it into multiple graphs, spreadsheets, or tables?
- Are the selected formats most conducive to communicating the message—in terms of clarity and complementing one another?
- Will any of this information mask, minimize, or detract from the clarity and precision of my message?
- What relationships among elements of the communication am I intending to portray (e.g., cause-and-effect, sequential)?
- Are there design considerations that will make the display more compelling, more original?

Step 5   Draft the Visualization
Draft the spreadsheet and graphics consistent with the answers to questions addressed in Steps 1 through 4. Use the answers from Step 2 as captions.

Step 6   Final Assessment
Use the same table as applied to the graphics from Minard, Snow, and Nightingale to assess the visualizations completed in Step 5.

Step 7   Make Any Needed Revisions

Using the assessment completed in Step 6, rework the graphs or spreadsheets until they meet the fundamental expectation for a successful visualization: *a precisely defined purpose and a purposeful depiction that delivers that purpose.*

Notes

1 Report of the President's Commission on the Accident at Three Mile Island: The Need for Change: The Legacy of TMI, October 30, 1979.
2 Report of the President's Commission.
3 Cliff Kuang, "Lessons from the Scariest Design Disaster in American History," Bookshelf, January 12, 2021, https://design.google/library/user-friendly.
4 International Atomic Energy Agency (IAEA), Control Room Systems Design for Nuclear Power Plants, IAEA-TECDOC-812, July 1995, https://inis.iaea.org/collection/NCLCollectionStore/_Public/27/002/27002051.pdf.
5 Report of the President's Commission.

6 U.S. Nuclear Regulatory Commission, Human Factors Evaluation of Control Room Design and Operator Performance at Three Mile Island—2 Final Report, NUREG 1270, January 1980, https://tmi2kml.inl.gov/Documents/2c-L2-NUREG/NUREGCR-1270,%20Vol.%201,%20Human%20Factors%20Evaluation%20of%20Control%20Room%20Design%20and%20Operator%20Performance%20at%20TMI-2%20(1980-01).pdf.

7 IAEA, "Control Room Systems Design."

8 Charles Joseph Minard, "Graphic Tables and Figurative Maps," trans. Dawn Finley, 1862, https://www.edwardtufte.com/tufte/minard-maps.

9 Minard, "Graphic Tables."

10 V. Chevallier, "The Life of Charles Edward Minard (1781–1870)," trans. Dawn Finley, 1871, https://www.edwardtufte.com/tufte/minard-obit.

11 Edward Tufte, *The Visual Display of Quantitative Information, 2nd ed.* (Cheshire, C.T.: Graphics Press, 2001).

12 Edward Tufte, *Beautiful Evidence* (Cheshire, C.T.: Graphics Press, 2006).

13 Chevallier, "The Life of Charles Edward Minard."

14 Chevallier, "The Life of Charles Edward Minard."

15 Stephen Talty, *Illustrious Dead: The Terrifying Story of How Typhus Killed Napolean's Greatest Army* (New York: Crown Publishers, 2009).

16 William Farr, *Report on the Mortality of Cholera in England, 1848–49* (London: W. Clowes and Sons, 1852), available at http://kora.matrix.msu.edu/files/21/120/15-78-12A-22-1852-GROReport48-49.pdf.

17 Farr, *Report on the Mortality of Cholera,* lxxiii–lxxvi.

18 "Cholera and the London Water Supply," *Supplement to the* Weekly Return, November 19, 1853, available at http://kora.matrix.msu.edu/files/21/120/15-78-126-22-1853-11-19-WRSupplementWater.pdf.

19 John Snow, "On the Chief Cause of the Recent Sickness and Mortality in the Crimea," *Medical Times and Gazette,* May 12, 1855, 457–458, http://johnsnow.matrix.msu.edu/work.php?id=15-78-48.

20 John Snow, *On the Modes of Communication of Cholera* (London: John Churchill, 1859), 75, available at http://kora.matrix.msu.edu/files/21/120/15-78-28-22-1849-08-29-MCC-a.pdf.

21 M. Eileen Magnello, "The Statistical Thinking and Ideas of Florence Nightingale and Victorian Politicians," *Radical Statistics* 102 (2010): 17–32.

22 Magnello, "The Statistical Thinking."

23 Harriet Martineau, *England and Her Soldiers* (London: Smith Elder & Co, 1859).

24 Martineau, *England and Her Soldiers; and Florence Nightingale, Mortality of the British Army* (London: Harrison and Son, 1858).

Chapter 5

Recognizing When Enough Is Enough

At the Library of Congress on the evening of March 24, 1983, President Ronald Reagan offered opening remarks for an exhibition depicting the life of the "American Cowboy":

> *If we understand this part of our history and our continuing fascination with it, we will better understand how our people see themselves and the hopes they have for America ... . Ideals of courageous and self-reliant heroes.. are the stuff of Western lore ... . Integrity, morality, and democratic values are the resounding themes.*[1]

As is evident, President Reagan was captivated by the stereotyped image of the American West of the 19th century and its legacy in shaping contemporary values and ideals. That portrayal of rugged individualism represents an idealized America that emerged with the 1820s publication of *The Prairie*—the first of James Fennimore Cooper's *Leatherstocking Tales*, intensified with the mid-century westward migration, and held sway early into the 20th century.

It is an image most effectively manufactured and marketed by Ned Buntline, who transformed William Frederick Cody—a hunter supplying buffalo meat to the army—into Buffalo Bill: Hunter, trapper, and Indian fighter. In dime store novels and his dramatic stage production, *Scout of the Prairie*, Buntline introduced Buffalo Bill—and life on the open range—to enthralled audiences across America and England.

Yet, while Buffalo Bill was a purposeful demonstration of myth-making, another enduring legend derives from a single event in American history that lasted all of 30 seconds.

In his 1931 biography, *Wyatt Earp: Frontier Marshall*, written in cooperation with Earp and published just two years after the marshal's death, Stuart Lake burnished that legend:

> Earps were in the vanguard of those hardy, self-reliant pioneers who led the course of empire across the wilderness. To an Earp, intrepid

DOI: 10.4324/9781003455585-6

confidence in his own strength, his own sagacity, his own courage, became a birthright.[2]

The genesis of that legend, the shootout at the OK Corral, occurred on October 26, 1881, a day, as described by *The Nugget*—one of two Tombstone, Arizona newspapers—"to be remembered as witnessing the bloodiest and deadliest street fight that has ever occurred in this place, or probably in the Territory."[3] Squaring off in the vacant lot adjacent to Camillus Fly's photography studio (across from but not actually in the OK Corral), the three Earp brothers (Wyatt, Virgil, and Morgan) accompanied by Doc Holliday met up with four "cowboys" (a term then used to denote outlaws): Ike and Billy Clanton and Frank and Tom McLaury.

Alerted to threats that the Clantons intended to shoot the Earps on sight, the four lawmen walked calmly down Fremont Street to the awaiting cowboys. Stopping about 10 feet from them, Virgil shouted: "Throw up your hands; I have come to disarm you!"

Almost instantaneously, a shot rang out. "Within 30 seconds six men had been shot, Billy Clanton and both McLaury brothers were dead or dying; Virgil and Morgan were seriously wounded, and Doc Holliday was slightly hurt. Wyatt was unscathed, as was Ike, the instigator of it all, who had run away when the shooting began."[4]

As reported in the October 27, 1881 issue of *The Tombstone Epitaph*, "the Marshal was entirely justified in his efforts to disarm these men, and that being fired upon they had to defend themselves which they did most bravely."[5] Humiliated, Ike filed a murder charge against Wyatt.

For the first two weeks of an inquest convened on October 31st, prosecution witnesses asserted the Earps instigated the shootout and had fired on unarmed men. Beginning on November 16th, the defense, leading off with Wyatt, highlighted the escalating "conspiracy to murder" the Earps; the cowboys' criminal history; and their repeated disregard for the ordinance making it "unlawful to carry ... any deadly weapon within the limits of said city of Tombstone."[6]

On November 30th, having given "patient attention to the hearing of evidence in this case," Judge Wells Spicer rendered his verdict: "There being no sufficient cause to believe ... Wyatt S. Earp and John H. Holliday guilty of the offense ... I order them to be released."[7] "No sufficient cause," as Spicer highlighted—in more than one instance—was largely a consequence of the prosecution's witnesses lacking credibility:

It is claimed by the prosecution that the deceased were shot while holding up their hands in obedience of the command of the chief of police, ... William Clanton was wounded on the wrist of the right hand on the first fire and thereafter used his pistol with his left. This wound is

such as could not have been received with his hands thrown up ... .
These ... facts, throw great doubt upon the correctness of the statement
of witnesses to the contrary.[8]

Most incredulous of the witnesses was Andy Behan, the Cochise County Sheriff. On the witness stand, misjudging when enough was enough, he became entrapped in a cascading series of falsehoods and exaggerations.

Whereas he had visited Virgil the night after the gunfight to tell him "You did perfectly right" (a statement independently corroborated), Behan manipulated and misrepresented facts to promote the impression the Earps, "spoiling for a fight," had committed premeditated murder. However, the more he dissembled, the less credible he became.

How, if the cowboys were unarmed, as Behan insisted, did they wound Virgil, Morgan, and Holliday? Was it conceivable, as Behan asserted, that in a fight he didn't "think ... lasted over 20 or 30 seconds," that "there was as many as eight or ten shots before [there were] arms in the hands of any of the McLaury or Clanton party"? Or was his representation of the first shot even feasible?

Although numerous witnesses confirmed Holliday alone carried a shotgun and despite the coroner having concluded the shot that killed Tom McLaury came from a shotgun, Behan insisted Holliday fired the first shots using his pistols. That act would have required Holliday, within seconds, to fire his pistols, drop them, retrieve the shotgun, and then shoot Tom McLaury.

With a single question during cross-examination, Wyatt's lawyer totally discredited Behan: "Is it not a fact that the first shot fired by Holliday was from a shotgun; that he then threw the shotgun down and drew the nickel-plated pistol from his person and then discharged the nickel-plated pistol?"[9] Behan, tacitly conceding his undoing, offered no response.

Disguising impressions as facts, promoting an inflated sense of self, and presenting information in both detail and volume beyond that warranted by the subject or the situation—a basic failure to acknowledge when enough is enough—Behan not only tanked the prosecution's case; he helped catapult Wyatt Earp into the foreground of American folklore.

We can assume most business professionals would never risk their careers by relying on blatant mischaracterizations of a situation or the purposeful dismissal of facts as evidenced in Behan's testimony; yet far too many professionals unintentionally manufacture circumstances that diminish their professional standing, reputations, and promotability by simply not knowing when enough is enough in a conversation, meeting, report, or presentation.

Going Over the Top

Although professionals are unlikely to rely on the kind of information manipulation exhibited by Behan, there are four common (often inadvertent) tendencies professionals can exhibit when not keenly acceding to the lessons we have been discussing in the preceding chapters—formulating a focused response to the assigned task and presenting it in targeted and tailored communications (text, oral, and visualized data) that ensure ease of management's comprehension:

- Pretension: Communications that reflect one's arrogance, designed not exclusively for communicating effectively, but for demonstrating how much you know or how smart you are;
- Attention: Communications that are littered with statements of your accomplishments and references to authority as a means to assert and amplify your importance and contentions;
- Detention: Introducing excessive detail; lingering unnecessarily on the obvious; or, simply, not ending when you've said all that needs to be said;
- Dissension: Becoming verbally combative rather than listening when challenged, creating a tension that is intended to serve only as a vehicle to "one up" everyone.

It is unlikely, considering these four categories, that you will not already be envisioning colleagues and managers who have demonstrated these traits and remembering situations in which you were held captive by their behaviors.

Given this commonly shared experience, we need only rely on brief summaries of such circumstances before exploring techniques to ensure we avoid being the source of such conduct.

Pretension

When practiced at a corporate level, pretention—or arrogance—translates into management-sanctioned dismissal and disdain for accepted norms and protocols. It is, to use a well-known example, a culture as exemplified by Enron, a major energy corporation that collapsed in 2001. The executives and staff believing themselves "The Smartest Guys in the Room," led to a progression from skirting accepted accounting practices to outright fraudulent trading schemes.[10] As a consequence, once the seventh largest company in the United States, Enron, within a single year, saw its stock prices plummet from $90 to 50 cents a share, erasing $67 billion of shareholder wealth, bankrupting numerous pension funds, wiping out life savings of thousands of individuals, and earning executives significant prison sentences.

At an individual level, as reported in a 2022 survey of some 1,900 workers conducted for the Society of Human Resource Management (SHRM), "arrogance" was among the top five most commonly cited "annoying behaviors" in the workplace—cited as just slightly less bothersome than "taking credit for the work of others" and "not doing their own work."[11]

At this individual level, as delineated by a group of psychologists from the University of Missouri, arrogance in the workplace can be manifested in three forms:

Individual arrogance = an overestimation of one's knowledge, limitations, or abilities.

Comparative arrogance = a sense or belief in one's superiority accompanied by an unwillingness to entertain the positions or perspectives of others.

Antagonistic arrogance = The purposeful disdain for others.[12]

Irrespective of which form is the underlying motivation, arrogance can become more than an annoyance to coworkers and management. Rather, overestimating one's knowledge, accompanied by an unwillingness to acknowledge the perspectives of colleagues, can, as the Enron example illustrates, contribute to instituting poor or imprudent business practices.

As example of a more common workplace scenario, as is a common practice, at one company monthly reports detailing cost and schedule performance were presented to assist senior management in identifying and prioritizing strategic business decisions. A critical component of these reports was a two- to three-sentence explanation of account variances—the differences between established budgets and costs incurred.

Despite being presented with strong arguments against changing the process, one manager—deeming herself an expert in management systems—instituted a set of 18 criteria each variance statement was now expected to be addressed by cost analysts in detail at every meeting. The result was more work for the staff preparing the reports; significant time diverted from other projects; and diminished value to the executives, now challenged to extract salient information. Rather than assisting in decision-making, the report now served principally to announce and enshrine the manager's arrogance.

Attention

Having recast variance statements into mini-treatises, the diminished usefulness of the reports was accompanied by the authoring manager's tedious and oft-repeated rationalization: "The regulators love our reports." While local management was now only minimally attentive to the reports and treated as if a secondary audience, the report's current incarnation had been hijacked using a variation of the fallacy of false authority.

In this fallacy, a generally well-known personality with little to no relevant expertise is used to endorse a product or concept (as in using ball players to advertise insurance plans). In this instance, the regulators, who had limited interest in or application for the reports, were not so much totally uninformed about the subject as they were distant—but influential—cousins.

Nevertheless, by introducing the oversight agency as the source of the revisions, the manager had negated any explicit internal challenge to the new format and, at the same time, had emboldened her to introduce a second major change to the monthly reporting regimen.

Compounding the weight of the regulator endorsement with the manager's demonstrated arrogance resulted in presentations during which the information density was so high (the pace so inappropriate) that little to no useful information could be isolated by the audience. The expanded variance statements were now accompanied by tables sporting as many as 50+ rows and 20 columns of numbers.

Detention

It's not hard to imagine the scene wherein an individual given to self-aggrandizement takes control of the forum. The presentation, already diminished in value, now focused as much attention on the manager's self-congratulatory comments and reminding everyone of the regulator's endorsement as it did on exploring subject matter central to shaping strategic decisions.

Yet, as arduous as the meetings had become, two actions by the manager further extended each meeting: (1) undue repetition of well-understood points the manager sought to impress upon the audience; and (2) despite the accompanying audience silence, numerous attempts by the manager to solicit response to strings of rhetorical questions.

Only after a lengthy detention had been served at each meeting was the audience released, often to the sounds of muttering about the declining quality of the material, the pretension of the speaker, and the amount of time wasted in meetings.

Dissension

Although insertion of the regulators into the conversation had effectively precluded any overt challenge to the revised format, that protection did not extend to independent auditors. When an auditor's report noted the presentations were only minimally contributing to corporate decision-making, antagonistic arrogance replaced the less combative arrogance previously exhibited, as voiced in the manager's written response to the audit report:

[I have] deep concerns regarding the merits of [the auditor's] ... methodology for conducting the audit, and the circumstances underlying the decision to conduct this audit and for what purpose ... .Furthermore, [findings] ... were based on the auditors' misapplication of the ... criteria, a misunderstanding of [our] ... procedures and, in many respects, are inconsistent with the auditors' own factual observations during the audit.

As might well be expected, the letter only served to escalate the problem: The regulator—who had hired the auditing firm—threatened to withhold funds pending a comprehensive re-evaluation of the company's entire performance management program. That review, in turn, generated an extensive corrective action plan that took the greater share of six months to implement.

Once fully implemented, the actions essentially realigned the program—shifting back to the original, streamlined version with the sole focus of answering management's information needs.

Bounding Communications

To avoid inadvertent demonstrations of arrogance, being labeled as someone demanding attention, routinely overextending interactions, or, worse, being dismissive of colleagues' efforts and perspectives, professionals need to employ techniques that demonstrate knowing when enough is enough—practices complementing the lessons of preceding chapters.

Simply stated, in each instance—whether an oral or written presentation—the basic strategy entails predefining the scope, level of detail, and sequencing of materials.

Yet, before we move into that discussion, as counterpoint to the poor behaviors just described, it is worthwhile to offer an example of the positive results derived when the goal of making management's jobs easier is accompanied by an appreciation of when enough is enough.

Demonstrating the Principle

Cooperatives originated in 1843 in Rochdale, England when "a few poor weavers out of employ, and nearly out of food and quite out of heart with the social state, met together to discover what they could do to better their industrial condition."[13] From that modest beginning, coops proliferated in the 1930s with the US Department of Agriculture initiative to promote the "electrification" of rural America.

With this major government funding came extensive accounting and reporting requirements, signified by "Form 7," a multi-page analysis of the coop's financial performance. Although completed by the coop's chief financial officer (CFO), the form must be signed by the Board of Directors—locally elected coop members—attesting to the coop's financial integrity.

The CFO's problem in this instance was how to give eight average citizens with little if any accounting knowledge sufficient insight to allow them while serving as board members to sign with confidence. His solution comprised two elements: (1) providing an appreciation of what was required in Form 7, which he accomplished by capturing the 86 required accounting categories on a single slide; and then (2) providing simple equations allowing board members to use the form to do their own confirmatory calculations of critical performance parameters such as "operating margins," the profit earned by the coop (Figure 5.1).

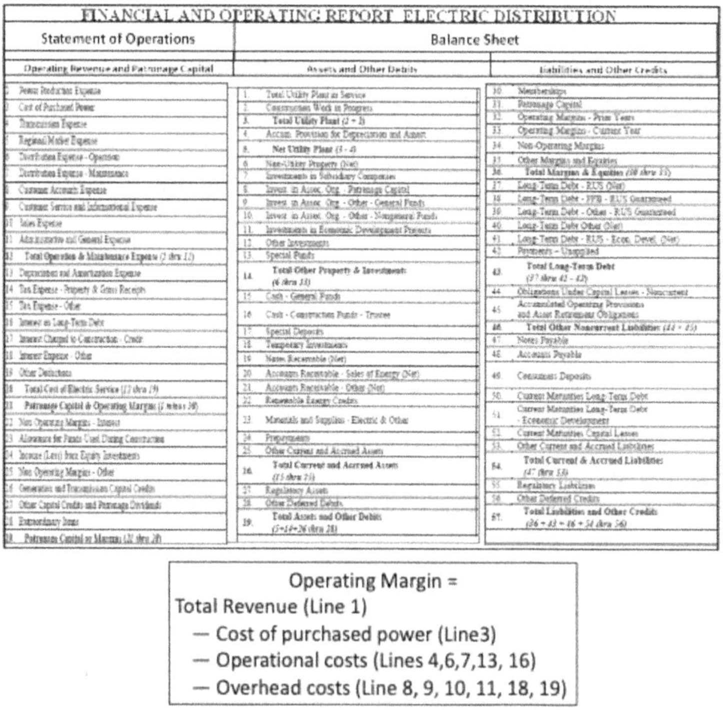
FINANCIAL AND OPERATING REPORT ELECTRIC DISTRIBUTION
Statement of Operations
Balance Sheet
Operating Margin =
Total Revenue (Line 1)
— Cost of purchased power (Line3)
— Operational costs (Lines 4,6,7,13, 16)
— Overhead costs (Line 8, 9, 10, 11, 18, 19)

Figure 5.1 Making Enough Count.

So, with that prescription for success—the alignment of information focus, level of specificity, and pace—let's examine the principal practices governing the necessary monitoring to ensure just the right amount and presentation of information in reports, presentations, and in face-to-face exchanges.

Keeping Reports Meaningful

In a lengthy written document (report or letter), much of the important information—the materials driving decisions—tends to unfold throughout the document, often with the most significant material withheld until the reader reaches the sections on conclusions and recommendations. Although managers could skip past all the intervening sections of the report—like turning to the final pages of a detective novel to find out who committed the crime—the answers would come with limited appreciation of the significance, application, or implications of the proposed actions.

Further, accepting this wading through detail as an appropriate business communication practice would directly contradict several of the lessons already considered in this text. In particular, the approach violates the rule of not making managers and executives work too hard to glean substance of keen interest or critical consequence.

The solution to this dilemma (too much information and not enough time) is primarily provided by a well written Executive Summary (or simply "Summary" in the case of lengthy letters), a synopsis at the beginning of the manuscript that synthesizes in abbreviated form the information central to decision-making.

In perhaps the most memorable advice regarding an Executive Summary, in the 1950s, Dupont corporation issued this report guidance to its engineering staff:

> The [Executive] Summary is addressed, above all, to the reader who must skim a hundred reports a day. He cares not a whit how you wound up to toss the egg but is intensely interested in what useful results were obtained when it hit the fan. Tell him that, and no more. He isn't going to throw any eggs himself, and he isn't going to advise anybody how to throw eggs. To him, the result and its implications are the important things ... .
>
> No matter how much it hurts, minimize the discussion of the motions that you went through in arriving at your conclusions, and keep your order of presentation logical rather than historical. The summary of a report is not an abridged narrative: it has to do with answers, not with plots. You can plot all you want to on your own time.[14]

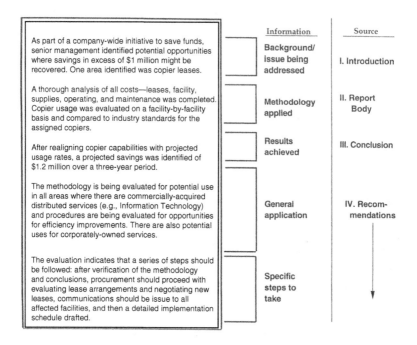

Figure 5.2 The Genesis and Substance of the Executive Summary.

Using the cost-saving initiative (copier reductions) discussed in Chapter 2 as an example, Figure 5.2 illustrates the derivation of an Executive Summary.

However, although the Executive Summary constitutes the main technique for efficiently presenting the essential substance of the report, it is not the only factor that may influence the report's reception and effectiveness. Rather, complete control and purposeful design must be exercised with each report section.

Misaligning the substance of the sections and their intended uses may diminish the report's value. As example, in one instance, an engineer was frustrated that his report—although presenting extensive research and valuable insights and conclusions—had twice been rejected by the regulator that had funded the work. The problem, as identified in a subsequent conversation with the regulator, was that the detail on methodology and background overwhelmed and "buried" the conclusions.

In this case, differentiating among the purposes of each report section made evident that shifting the detail into appendices would retain the specificity expected by the author's scientific colleagues, but would also make the information in the body of value to the decision-makers more pronounced, accessible, and more easily implemented. The lesson being that each section of

Table 5.1 Business Report Structure

Component	Purpose
Title	Assist in report retrieval and correspondence to other reports
Executive Summary	Highlight substance critical to decision-making, support easy navigation
Table of Contents	Allow ease of navigation; clarify relationship among sections and subsections
Introduction	Establish basic framework of research and report organization
Body	Provide context for the research—history, methodology, and limitations
Conclusions	Explain findings in a sequence consistent with themes developed in body
Recommendations	Translate conclusions into specific courses of assigned actions
Appendices	Support independent evaluation and substantiation of results and conclusions
Distribution List	Ensure receipt by appropriate sponsors, management, and colleagues

the report (as summarized in Table 5.1) has an explicit purpose and audience that defines the scope and appropriate information tailoring required if the report is to merit the desired value, impact, and recognition.

Targeting Presentations

In essence, presentations and long reports share a common trait: Both use compilations of information sequenced according to standard organizational patterns to present an argument or theme. However, aside from the greater reliance on the visualization of information, presentations tend to provide a more direct narrative of what happened, why, and what needs to be done.

To develop this cohesive narrative, rather than initially pondering the phrasing of the title or the proof to be provided, the effort begins with casting the concluding slide. The goal of focusing on the conclusion is three-fold: (1) forcing the articulation of precisely what is to be accomplished, (2) concentrating the focus and setting boundaries on the breadth and depth of information needed to sustain the assertions, and (3) distinguishing the substance and sequencing of each slide. In other words, the conclusion slide is the formulation of precisely what is enough.

Using the conclusion slide as a roadmap then establishes the basis for proceeding logically and with confidence through the development of the remainder of the presentation:

- The title slide is developed as a variation of the principal assertion cited on the concluding slide.

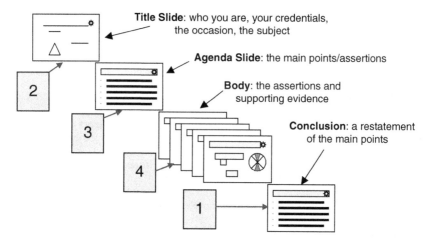

Figure 5.3 The Strategy and Development of Presentations.

- The agenda slide profiles and forecasts the substance of the conclusion slide.
- Each of the slides in the body
  - takes its title from,
  - is presented in the same sequence as, and
  - amplifies one or more bullets presented on the conclusion slide (Figure 5.3).

Face Time

Whether working in the office, participating virtually, running into colleagues outside of work, or representing the company at a conference or sales meeting, your verbal exchanges provide critical statements about your professional abilities, problem-solving, analytical capability, and personality. Yet the expectations for meetings differ appreciably from those governing interactions between individuals.

Meetings

Formal business meetings are easy to negotiate owing to the fact that there are well-established logistical protocols (agendas, time allowances, assigned and unassigned roles) and behavioral expectations. Generally, to be considered professional requires little more than a willingness to adhere to these protocols and behaviors (Table 5.2).

Table 5.2 Meeting Predicates and Etiquette

What Is Expected of You	What Is Not Appreciated

• Act in the best interests of the team and the organization you represent:
  • Measure success by what the team accomplishes,
  • Bring your experience, expertise, and judgment to every meeting,
  • Be assertive, but not to the exclusion of listening carefully,
  • Acknowledge sound ideas and opinions—even if conflicting with your own,
  • Only introduce relevant data and information and present it concisely,
  • Strive for the optimum answer—address challenges, obstacles, and alternatives,
  • Encourage participation by everyone,
  • Adhere to the established protocols,
  • Never lose focus on the team's goals.
	• Don't talk just to hear yourself speak or to try to impress everyone! In particular don't
	  • Hog the stage or withdraw from the discussion,
	  • Repeat in detail what has already been said, clarify points already clear, or ask questions already answered,
	  • Present additional examples after a statement has been amply debated,
	  • Rubberstamp statements simply because they are offered by someone more senior,
	  • Bring up peripheral issues that detract from the primary focus,
	  • Ignore visual cues suggesting you are being too long-winded, intrusive, or off the point,
	  • Send visual cues or demonstrate behaviors indicating a disinterest in or boredom with other speakers or the meeting.

Conversations, on the other hand, demand more diligence of the professional who is intending to make and maintain good impressions and positive relationships.

Conversations

As with meetings, the same rules apply as regards not being boorish, self-consumed, or overbearing. However, whereas in meetings, as we just noted, protocols for achieving behaviors are distributed among participants and overseen by a facilitator, in conversations each participant becomes immediately and personally accountable (in full or in part) for the substance, flow, and conclusion of the exchange—a function described by one study as owning a "bundle of complex tasks":

> Conversation is common, but it is not simple ... To converse, people must generate and comprehend language in real time, alternate turns in rapid sequence, infer what their partners know and don't know and want to know, remember what has and hasn't been said, and much more. [They] seem simple only because humans generally do them well and fail to notice when they do them poorly.[15]

In conducting a business conversation, as the open literature amply describes, professionals are charged with ensuring the appropriate attitudes, impressions, and responses are conveyed through visual cues, language, and verbal responses. However, what remains largely unattended is an additional responsibility that is equally if not more challenging: Assessing when and how to conclude the conversation.

It is, in the words of the study just quoted, a "coordination problem" complicated by the fact that information is "kept secret" regarding each participant's goal and "humans are bad at solving the problem." As the review of 922 conversations concluded, conversations "almost never ended when both conversants wanted them to and rarely ended when even one conversant wanted them to." Moreover, the study found "not one shred of support" for that assumption that exchanges served as a "harmonizing process that brings conversants' desires into alignment and allows them to construct a mutual desire to end at roughly the same time."

Adding perspective to these insights, a second study identified that lacking a mutually agreed conclusion to the conversation, individuals relied on a range of verbal and non-verbal gambits to encourage ending or actually terminating the exchange:

- Changing subjects: Introducing a new topic as a prelude to concluding the conversation
- Closing statements: Making an explicit concluding remark, e.g., "I have to go"
- Excuses: Assigning external reasons to end the conversation, e.g., another meeting
- Getting third-party help: Soliciting participation by an additional individual
- Non-responsiveness: Fading from the conversation, e.g., passively agreeing
- Polite hinting: Signaling verbally, e.g., "We need to do this again soon"
- Restlessness: Sending non-verbal cues, e.g., yawning, looking away, fidgeting
- Rudeness: Using brusque language or tones, then abandoning the conversation
- Turning the table: Transferring the responsibility to conclude the conversation, e.g., "didn't you say something about having another meeting?"
- Vanishing: Simply quitting and walking away from the discussion.[16]

Considering these concluding devices might suggest the best alternatives were either to use "polite hinting" because it is ostensibly the least objectionable in terms of reception by a colleague or manager, or "closing statements" because they are the most expedient means of ending the conversation. However, more than likely, using any of these devices risks being considered unprofessional, could prove damaging to relationships, and likely diminishes the potential benefit that might have been derived from the conversation.

Instead, the only appropriate strategy should focus on ensuring those goals—the "secret" information—are made known and accommodated in the conversation.

The success of a conversation is dependent on the same principal factor associated with the success of any business communication: A crisp, agreed-upon problem statement and a straightforward presentation of the information essential to its resolution. In conversations that requirement translates into establishing a basic alignment of the participants' goals and acknowledgment of any limitations such as time constraints. It is essentially the equivalent of beginning with the conclusion slide when defining the intent and scope of a presentation. And, as with presentations, parameters can often be mutually established with as little as a single sentence. For example: "I need to talk with you about the schedule for the new project, but I only have 30 minutes."

When a conversation has already started and then it becomes apparent there are divergent goals or expectations, a secondary approach should be employed. Rather than remaining silent, politely inquire about whether there is a shared understanding of what precipitated the conversation. As example, when opportunity arises, a phrase such as the following will put the conversation back on track without embarrassing or insulting the other participant(s): "I'm sorry, but I thought we were going to discuss the timing of the next project?"

As the patterns demonstrate, irrespective of the form of the communication—whether report, presentation, meeting, or conversation—the means to ensure you do not exceed the point at which you are belaboring the subject, holding your audience captive, or having strayed far from the central point—is only achieved by keeping the end in mind.

The meeting's agenda, the report's executive summary, the presentation's concluding slide, and the articulation of participants' goals for a discussion are all targeted at the same thing: Establishing boundaries for and the point of conclusion for business communications. Common sense, with a little help from these devices, is the only means to know for certain when enough is enough.

Notes

1 Ronald Reagan, "Remarks at the Opening of 'The American Cowboy' Exhibit at the Library of Congress." March 24, 1983. https://www.reaganlibrary.gov/archives/speech/remarks-opening-american-cowboy-exhibit-library-congress

2 Stuart N. Lake, *Wyatt Earp: Frontier Marshall* (Pocket Books: New York, 1994).

3 "Shootout in the OK Coral Tome Line in Tombstone," November 1, 2012. http://deadwoodsdnow.blogspot.com/2012/11/1881-tombstone-epitaph-newspaper-shoot.html

4 Steven Lubet, *Murder in Tombstone: The Forgotten Trial of Wyatt Earp* (Yale University Press: New Haven, 2004).

5 "Yesterday's Tragedy: Three Men Hurled Into Eternity in the Duration of a Moment" Tombstone Daily Epitaph—October 27, 1881
http://law2.umkc.edu/faculty/projects/ftrials/earp/epitaph.html

6 Kimberly Carlton Bonner, "A Historic Acquittal Re-Examined: Would the Earps and Doc Holliday Escape Indictment under the Modern Grand Jury System?" *Journal of the West* 56, no. 3 (Summer 2017): 60–84. ttps://searchworks.stanford.edu/articles/31h__133125414

7 Douglas O. Linder, "Decision of Judge Wells Spicer after the Preliminary Hearing in the Earp-Holliday Case," Famous Trials, https://famous-trials.com/earp/501-spicerdecision

8 Ibid.

9 Douglas O. Linder, "Testimony of Sheriff John H. Behan in the Preliminary Hearing in the Earp-Holliday Case Heard before Judge Wells Spicer," Famous Trials, https://famous-trials.com/earp/510-behantestimony

10 Bethany McLean and Peter Elkind, *The Smartest Guys in the Room, The Amazing Rise and Scandalous Fall of Enron* (New York: Portfolio Trade, 2003).

11 Kathy Gurchiek, "Most Annoying Co-Worker, Manager Habits," SHRM, March 17, 2022. https://www.shrm.org/hr-today/news/hr-news/pages/most-annoying-coworker-manager-habits.aspx

12 Nelson Cowan, Eryn J. Adams, Sabrina Bhangal, "Foundations of Arrogance: A Broad Survey and Framework for Research," *Review of General Psychology* 23, no. 4 (2019): 425–443. https://memory.psych.missouri.edu/assets/doc/articles/2019/Cowan-et-al-Review-of-General-Psychology-2019-arrogance.pdf

13 George Jacob Holyoake, *The History of the Rochdale Pioneers* (London: George Allen and Unwin Ltd, 1918).

14 "The Dratted) P(rogress) Report." Report No, DP-00. E.I. Dupont & Nemours, Inc. Savannah River Laboratory: Aiken, SC., July 12, 1954.

15 Adam Mastroianni, Daniel Gilbert, Gus Cooney, Timothy Wilson, "Do Conversations End When People Want Them To?" Proceedings of the National Academy of Sciences of the United States of America, March 1, 2021. https://www.pnas.org/doi/full/10.1073/pnas.2011809118

16 Josephine Bao-Sun Cein, Conversational Retreat Typology, Masters' Thesis. San Jose University, 1989 https://scholarworks.sjsu.edu/cgi/viewcontent.cgi?article=4055&context=etd_theses

Chapter 6

Reasoning Logically

In 1543 when Copernicus published *On the Revolutions of the Heavenly Spheres*, Andreas Osiander became what one scholar referred to as "the greatest villain in the history of science."[1] He earned that distinction by adding an introduction to the book asserting Copernicus' proposed concept—the earth circling the sun—was not scientific fact, but, rather, a hypothesis to be treated skeptically. "[I]t is the job of the astronomer to use painstaking and skilled observation in gathering together the history of the celestial movements, and then—since he cannot by any line of reasoning reach the true causes of these movements—to think up or construct whatever causes or hypotheses he pleases such that, by the assumption of these causes, those same movements can be calculated."[2] Yet, Copernicus was not the first nor the last astronomer to receive a hostile reception for advocating the heliocentric theory of the universe.

A disciplined study of astronomy begins with the Babylonians, who, in about 10th century BCE, recorded the rising and setting of stars and constellations. By the 6th century BCE, Ptolemy and the Greeks had advanced the science, however, erroneously positioning the earth as the center of the universe. At the time, Aristarchus of Samos presented a solitary dissenting opinion, which, as recounted years later in Archimedes' *The Sand Reckoner*, remained for centuries a discredited hypothesis: "Aristarchus of Samos brought out a book ... . His hypotheses are that the fixed stars and the sun remain unmoved, that the earth revolves about the sun in the circumference of a circle, the sun lying in the middle of the orbit ... . Now it is easy to see that this is impossible."[3]

Inheriting this heliocentric argument, Galileo became the next major voice following Copernicus to proffer the theory. However, unlike Copernicus, who held off publication until shortly before his death rather than face the anticipated ridicule, Galileo met challengers head-on—often instigating confrontation.

Learning of the invention, in 1609, Galileo began constructing several generations of telescopes—achieving significant magnification in his third

DOI: 10.4324/9781003455585-7

attempt. Nonetheless, skeptics, many of whom refused even to look through a telescope, were unwilling to use the capability to assess the validity of the observations announced in Galileo's 1610 publication, *Starry Messenger*.

Even the least problematic of his discoveries—that the moon's surface was not smooth, but, rather, "rough and uneven and, just as the face of the Earth itself, crowded everywhere with prominences, deep chasms, and sinuosities"—was dismissed.[4] However, the majority of the acrimony was reserved for the most radical of his discoveries.

Not only did the discovery of Jupiter's moons demonstrate earth was not unique within the cosmos. Establishing that Jupiter's moons were traveling along with it in its orbit penetrated a centuries-old challenge to heliocentrism: If the earth is moving in space, shouldn't our moon continually get farther away?

Given the immediate popularity of Galileo's manuscript (selling out its first printing of 500 copies in a single week), it could not go unanswered by its detractors, whose challenges took several forms:

- Appeals to Common sense: Anyone can watch the sun rising in the morning, moving overhead at noon, and then setting in the evening.
- Attacks on the Reasoning: A cannonball whether fired to the east or west achieves the same distance. If the earth is moving, shouldn't the distances achieved be different?
- Citing Contradictions with Scripture: At the battle of Gibeon, "the sun stood still, and the moon stopped" (Joshua 10:13).

Having thus far failed to discredit Galileo, the skeptics personalized the scripturally based arguments. In his pamphlet, *Against the Motion of the Earth*, Ludovico delle Colombe, an astronomer with whom Galileo regularly clashed, led the *ad hominem* assault:

> *Could those poor fellows [heliocentrics] perhaps have recourse to an interpretation of scripture different than the literal interpretation? Definitely not, because all theologians, without exception, say that when Scripture can be understood literally, it ought never be interpreted differently.*[5]

Goaded by these taunts, Galileo was drawn away from his mathematical and scientific objections. Instead, although until that time the church had modestly (if not publicly) encouraged him to seek further proofs, had asserted no claims of infallibility, nor issued sanctions against him, Galileo sought "to make the words of scripture subservient to the axioms he laid down."[6]

In a widely circulated letter, Galileo first attempted to bind the role of scriptures: "Holy Scripture is solely to persuade men of those articles and propositions which are necessary for their salvation and which, being beyond the scope of human reasoning, could not be made credible to us by science or by any other means." As such, scriptures, he contended, "should be brought into scientific disputes only as a last resort."[7]

Intensifying the challenge, Galileo entered the realm of Biblical interpretation, suggesting scripture's few "scattered references" to science or astronomy confirmed the Bible's authors' intent to exclude matters within human reason: "For if the sacred writers had intended to persuade the people of the order of the motions of heavenly bodies, they would not have said so little about them."[8]

It followed, he reasoned, that it would be a "serious and frequent," error "to insist always on the literal meaning of the words, for this can lead not only to many contradictions but also to grave heresies and blasphemies." Illustrating such errors, Galileo proceeded to refute the theologians' interpretation of Joshua 10:13, offering a reinterpretation that "clearly demonstrates the impossibility of the Aristotelian and Ptolemaic world system, and on the contrary fits perfectly well with the system of Copernicus."[9]

This deepening rift with the church reached a peak in a letter Galileo sent to the Grand Duchess Christina in 1613. In a single sentence that well may have provoked the church to act, Galileo outrightly defied church authority: "The intention of the Holy Spirit is to teach us how one goes to heaven, not how the heaven goes!"[10] Shortly thereafter, in 1613, two propositions of censure were filed against him by the church: One for contending the sun is the "center of the world"; the second for contending the earth is not. As a consequence, Galileo was summoned to the court where he agreed to "abandon" his theory and "abstain altogether from teaching or defending his opinion."[11] However, Galileo's pugnacious nature ultimately resurfaced.

Following meetings in 1624 with Pope Urban II, an old school friend, Galileo was granted permission to write a defense of Copernicus on condition his theories remained hypothetical. In 1632, Galileo published *A Dialogue About the Two Chief World Systems*. In that text, three friends debate the nature of the universe: Salviati—a surrogate for Copernicus; Sagredo—an undecided individual; and Simplicio (implying simple-minded)—a geocentrist. Throughout the text, Simplicio's deflated and ridiculed arguments that man cannot "know how the world really is" echo and are soon identified by clerics as the exact positions voiced by the Pope during the 1624 discussions.

The Pope, who was not amused, withdrew both further support and protection for Galileo. Consequently, on June 22, 1633, Galileo, having been tried by the Holy Office of the Inquisition, was convicted of heresy, forced publicly to recant his theories, and confined for the remainder of his days to his house in Florence.

The Substance of Argument

Labeled a "myth" of the church's "supposed rejection of scientific progress" by Pope Paul II in 1992, Galileo's condemnation should, as this short history suggests, be more accurately understood as the consequence of a poorly waged argument.[12] Prior to Galileo angering the Pope, the Church had sought to dissuade him from advocating unproven hypotheses, not convict him of heretical teachings. Indicative of this intent, when censuring him, the 1613 tribunal did not declare him a heretic, but, rather, required he "abandon" his two "opinions" (the sun, not the earth, was the center of the universe) because they were, respectively, "foolish and absurd," and "erroneous in faith."[13]

However, failing to differentiate between reason and logic, Galileo's encounters with other astronomers and the church continued to veer into presenting hypotheses as proofs, relying on confirmation biases, and exchanging opinions rather than examining assumptions.

All these errors in creating and sustaining a cogent argument are considerations professionals need to understand and control if they are to be highly persuasive through reasoning logically (or logically reasoning) with counterparts and management.

Logic versus Reason

At the most fundamental level, the inability of the church and Galileo to reconcile their conflicting positions was an issue of logic versus reasoning. Theologians at the time operated on the belief that the scriptures presented absolute, scientific proofs; Galileo, as they perceived, relied on assumptions, inferences, and extrapolations. Allowed opportunity to present further "demonstration" in support of his theory, Galileo could not provide such absolute and verifiable proof. Rather, he sought to change the basis by which his conclusions should be measured, expecting theologians to deny the frame of reference that governed their thinking.

Just as claiming an idea is not the same as proving it, telling people their thinking is misguided is not generally the most persuasive strategy. Proof requires a line of argument that is clear, developed with the audience's perspective in mind, and designed consistent with the demands of the circumstance in which the argument is being presented.

To accomplish these ends, analyses often presume that the foundation for examining argument must lie with the study of logic and the formalism of syllogisms. However, that thinking is neither immediately applicable to the world of business nor in keeping with our goals here of concentrating on the practical lessons of value to professionals.

Accordingly, rather than enter into a lengthy discussion discerning the distinct domains of logic and reason, let me offer a simple illustration that will firmly and indelibly establish the difference.

Supposedly (a fact I have never been able to confirm), in the 1950s, the written test for a New York State driver's license had the following question:

Approaching from different directions, an ambulance, a police car, a fire engine, and a mail truck arrive at precisely the same moment at a four-way intersection controlled by stop signs. The fire engine, police car, and ambulance each have their lights and sirens on. Who has the right of way?

The correct answer at that time was the mail truck: It was the only Federal vehicle. That answer is the logical choice: It follows an established and inviolable rule that Federal jurisdiction takes precedence over local activities. In contrast, a reasonable answer would be to choose any of the other three vehicles engaged in response to an emergency.

In business, only machines and computers function logically (i.e., invariably according to fixed controls and rules). People in business, it is to be assumed, act reasonably. Making a successful, persuasive argument, therefore, begins with understanding how people reach decisions and then how to construct an argument most likely to solicit the desired response.

Decision-Making and the Logic of Argument

In 1910, Thomas Dewey, a professor of philosophy at Columbia University, published a small volume, *How We Think*, that defined the essential framework people use to make decisions. As he articulated, decisions are reached according to a sequence of "five logically distinct steps: (i) a felt difficulty; (ii) its location and definition; (iii) suggestion of possible solutions; (iv) development by reasoning of the bearings of the suggestion; (v) further observation and experiment leading to its acceptance or rejection; that is, the conclusion of belief or disbelief."[14]

Driven by a philosophy that placed experience as the "ultimate authority on knowledge and conduct," Dewey's structure, as he illustrated using a range of situations from "rudimentary to more complicated cases of reflection," defined the basic pathway we use when making decisions. As a first step a "difficulty" is identified. Thereafter, hypotheses are posited from which alternative solutions are identified, prioritized, or—if impractical or incomplete—rejected. Then the alternatives are assessed—their fit, consequences, practicality, and ease of

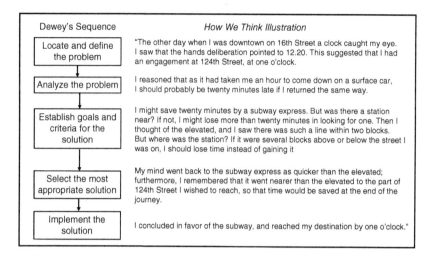

Figure 6.1 Illustration of the Decision-Making Sequence.

implementation—and the most appropriate solution is selected and implemented. (Figure 6.1 illustrates this process using one of the "rudimentary" examples provided in Dewey's text.)

Yet, in laying out the basic framework, Dewey—who focused most intently on students—does not provide sufficient definition to the sequence to allow it—unaided—to provide an appropriate framework for application within a business environment. Rather, as he explained, the "disciplined, or logically trained, mind … is the mind able to judge how far each of these steps needs to be carried in any particular situation. No cast-iron rules can be laid down." As he further explained, the "logically-trained mind" must ascertain and deliver the premises, comprising "grounds, foundations, [and] bases" that "underlie, uphold, and support the conclusion."[15]

The means to complement Dewey's decision-making sequence—delineating these components underpinning the conclusion and, at the same time, providing further visualizing of the substance of argument—was provided almost four decades later with the 1959 publication of Stephen Toulmin's, *An Introduction to Reasoning*.

As Toulmin explains, arguments comprise six elements:

- Claims: The statement of the thesis being argued. "When we embark on an argument, there is always a 'destination' we are invited to arrive at."
- Grounds: The facts or evidence used to provide or sustain the argument, the "underlying foundation" necessary if the claim is "to be accepted as solid and reliable."

- Warrants: The assumptions on which the claim is based. The means used to "justify the move from the grounds to the claim," the "road ... you take to get from the starting point to the destination."
- Backing: Statements that provide support and demonstrate the claim is solid and reliable. Backup may be needed to substantiate the warrant, grounds, and/or rebuttal, recognizing that "Warrants themselves cannot be taken wholly on trust."
- Rebuttals: Counterarguments or clarifications denoting the circumstances under which the argument does not hold true. "Does this route take us to the required destination securely and reliably?"
- Qualifiers: Statements that clarify the strength of the argument or that propose the conditions under which the argument holds true. "Just how reliably does the warrant lend weight to the given step from grounds to claim?"[16]

These components, as illustrated in Figure 6.2, depict the pathway from warrant through to the claim, substantiated by the appropriate level of support and a specifically defined degree of confidence in the conclusion. As the figure makes evident, not only does the depiction expand on and provide the needed amplification to Dewey's sequence; it provides a system for assessing both the process of decision-making and the elaboration of the underlying substance of the argument being presented. It also forges a unique bridge between the absolutes of logic and the representation of how people frame arguments and how business discussions unfold—relying on probabilities, hunches, expectations, and—most commonly—experience.

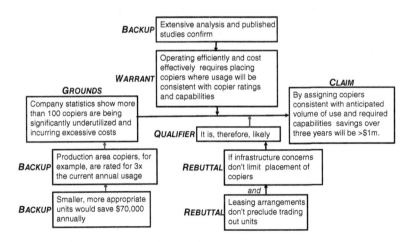

Figure 6.2 Illustration of Toulmin's Structure of Argument.

Taken together, the three principal components identified by Toulmin in this structure—warrant, grounds, and claim—are, in cases where the conclusion does not require further substantiation, equivalent to a basic syllogism: The three components of Toulmin's structure corresponding to the syllogism's major premise, minor premise, conclusion.

Highlighting this relationship, Toulmin points out that: "Rather than Logic and Rhetoric being rivals, offering competing recipes for judging the merits or defects in our reasoning, the considerations they focus on are complementary." Were the thought expressed as an equation, it might be stated as:

Rhetoric = Logical Representation + Substantiation

And, as Toulmin aptly concludes: "Once we understand what is at issue in any piece of argumentation, we can ask what data its claims rest on, how solidly the data support it, and how far the resulting claims carry conviction."[17]

Of significant importance in a business context is Toulmin's clarification that his framework for visualizing argument "is not a way of arriving at ideas but rather a way of testing ideas critically." It is, as he further elaborates, a means to examine "those utterances that succeed or fail only to the extent that they can be 'supported' by arguments, reasoning, evidence, or the like carrying the reader or hearer along with them only because they have such a 'rational foundation.'" In other words, whereas a syllogistic formula works with universally accepted truths, it will not provide the depth of analysis to assess arguments common to the world of business in which discussions involve validating theories and devising strategies to improve operational performance, efficiencies, or market position.

Although the breadth of contemporary business precludes any single, definitive statement that would encompass the ways in which reasoning is applied, credible generalizations can be made regarding typical characteristics governing arguments when viewed in terms of Toulmin's elements of argument:

- Warrants express the opportunity to improve profits, increase efficiency, create market stability, and minimize operational and financial risk;
- Claims tend to concentrate on statements asserting the appropriateness of pursuing proposals;
- Grounds present data that allow for comprehensive assessment of proposals;
- Qualifiers tend to define levels of confidence, probability of risks, and areas of uncertainty associated with the proposal, e.g., cost vs benefit, operational downtime, commercial viability;
- Rebuttals come in the form of alternative solutions that may be less risky, more profitable, easier to implement, or, as is often the case in large organizations, competing perspectives voiced by other organizations within the company;

- Backing is driven by circumstance—the types and extent of supporting detail needed as regards the warrant, grounds, and/or the rebuttals—e.g., explaining magnitude of risks, anticipated profit margins, schedule projections, or modeling results.

Further portraying the reality of how subjects are argued and business decisions are reached, elements of Dewey's sequence and of Toulmin's structure of argument may be implicit rather than explicit (i.e., stated or not stated). In the case of Dewey's sequence, the statement of goals is often understood and therefore not articulated. Similarly, in Toulmin's structure, warrants are often assumed, which, in turn, means the associated backing may also remain unstated. Moreover, complex arguments may entail multiple warrants—sometimes layered in support of fully developing a single assertion, sometimes in parallel when multiple warrants are required to establish the reliability of a claim.

It is the unstated assumptions that, for instance, allow economists to arrive at different determinations regarding the likelihood of an impending recession. That is why it is essential to be able to visualize the unstated foundations of many business arguments and decisions.

Equally important to revealing underlying assumptions in the visualization of argument is confirmation that all components of the argument—including the substantiation provided by the grounds and backing—directly contribute to demonstrating the certainty of the claim. If not, or if the argument does not sufficiently substantiate the claim, issues arise—including doubts regarding the integrity of the claim and, potentially, doubts about the individual making the claim.

If we now return momentarily to Galileo, we may more clearly envision the problem he encountered in trying to gain acceptance of his theory. His warrant (the sun was the center of the universe) and proof of his claim (the earth circles the sun) both rested solely on the grounds of his observations of the behavior of Jupiter's moons, with backing restricted to mathematical calculations intelligible only to other mathematicians. Relying on this limited foundation while allowing no qualifiers, summarily dismissing all rebuttals, and mistakenly veering into theological arguments, Galileo was unsuccessfully attempting to draw a straight line from warrant to claim.

Unfortunately for Galileo, given the technological limitations of the early 17th century, there was little else he was able to offer. Without additional evidence, Galileo's assertions relied on the willingness of his contemporaries, his colleagues, and the church to suspend their disbelief and abandon the orthodoxy that had governed the science of astronomy for centuries.

Although in 1758 the church tacitly acknowledged the science by lifting its ban on books teaching the heliocentric model, it was not until 1939 before Pope Pius XII acclaimed Galileo a "hero of science." It was only then, when reasoning became indisputable, and the church sought to forego further perceptions of the church's disavowal of science, that Galileo's reputation was redeemed.

With this introduction into the inherent challenges in persuading others—particularly in circumstances where the audience is not necessarily inclined to your position—we can now better appreciate the means of developing a persuasive argument.

Putting the Models into Practice

Several decades later, building on what he referred to as Dewey's "description" of how individuals "systematically think their way through to a decision," Alan Monroe, a speech professor at Purdue University, provided a "dependable psychological basis" on which to frame persuasive presentations. By "adhering to [a] general progression from question to answer or from problem to solution ... you can develop your appeals along the thought-line that most people are accustomed to following." Designed as a persuasive strategy, his "Motivated Sequence" thereby provided the framework for effectively synthesizing the work of both Dewey and Toulmin.

As Monroe detailed in his text, *The Principles of Speech Communication*, the sequence comprises five steps:

1   Attention Step—Locating and Defining the Problem: At this stage, the precise subject of consideration is identified. As we have emphasized in this text, without an exact definition of the problem's scope, specificity, and limits, there is little chance for achieving an adequate and satisfying solution.
2   Need Step—Analyzing the Problem: The principal part of this step involves an analysis of existing conditions including causes and implications. Until all the symptoms are accounted for, this step remains incomplete—and likely to result in a less than satisfactory solution.
3   Satisfaction Steps—Establishing Goals: With the problem's scope and causes known, criteria can be posited by which to assess the adequacy and appropriateness of potential solutions.
4   Visualization Step—Finding the Best Solution: Using the defined criteria, alternatives can be evaluated, their relative strengths determined, and a best (or preferred) solution selected.
5   Action Step—Putting the Best Solution into Operation: At this point, all that remains is to decide on the most appropriate means of implementation. Once determined and the plan implemented, the process is complete.[18]

Table 6.1 Aligning Form and Reasoning

Organizational Framework	Alignment with Decision-Making Sequence	Alignment with Elements of Reasoning
I Attention	Locate and define the problem	Warrant(s)
II Need	Analyze the problem	Grounds Backing
III Satisfaction	Establish goals and criteria for the solution	Grounds Backup
IV Visualization	Select the most appropriate solution	Grounds/Rebuttals/Qualifiers
V Action Step	Implement the solution	Claim(s)

By integrating this process by which people arrive at decisions with understanding of the structure of argument provides a means for developing and for assessing persuasively structured communications, whether presentations, letters, or reports. In each case, the general framework remains the same; it is the disciplined tailoring of the evidence—establishing the grounds, qualifiers, backing, and rebuttals—that delivers the substantiated, convincing, and "rational foundation" for the claim (Table 6.1).

In Chapter 4, we outlined the organization of various forms of communication, including discussion of the alignment of structure and reasoning in the development of presentations. Now, with insights provided by Dewey, Toulmin, and Monroe, we can also make evident how the sequencing of information can be employed to enhance the strength of the reasoning and the persuasiveness of the argument in narrative communications (e.g., letters, reports, proposals) (Table 6.2).

Table 6.2 Design of a Persuasive Document

Step	Principal Elements	Argument Summary
Attention	• opening statements	The power supply in this city is becoming increasingly inadequate given population growth. We need to expand reliance on hydroelectric power; it is safe, clean, economical, and renewable.
Need	• problem statement • illustration of seriousness • ramifications	There is an urgent need for more power. Last year we had 14 serious blackouts. Other fuel sources are less accessible in our area and less economical. Coal is 6 times more expensive and is rising at 12%/year. Wind and solar can't provide necessary capacity.

(Continued)

Table 6.2 (Continued)

Step	Principal Elements	Argument Summary

Satisfaction	• statement
	• explanation
	  • evidence
	  • theoretical
	    demonstration
	  • practical experience
	• answering objections
		We must get behind our state's energy program. A single dam will sustain the city for the next 20 years. In comparison, building a nuclear power or coal plant will cost 3x as much. Also, as shown in the table below, safety and environmental issues make these options untenable. Even objections like adverse impacts on the fishing industry can be readily and economically mitigated. As nearby states have demonstrated, hydroelectric power is the only sustainable and renewable long-term energy solution.

Visualization	• positive effects • negative effects	Here are the major benefits we will realize from building a dam—sufficient energy now and in the future, increasing the likelihood of securing major industrial growth, quality of life, and a healthier environment. Without the answer to our energy problems, the decline in our economy and the lost industrial opportunities will continue.
Action	• Concluding statement	If we are always to have the power we need, you should write to your congressman and to the Council on Environmental Quality to tell them to vote yes on Senate Bill 1002.

Tools to Assess the Argument

Aligning structure and reasoning also provides a keener ability to assess the cogency of argument and to understand the principal fallacies that lessen the integrity or reliability of claims being made. In that regard, we can consider fallacies, not as the esoterica of logic courses, but rather from the practical standpoint of how they affect the integrity of three specific sets of components within the argument's structure: (1) claims and warrants, (2) grounds and backing, or (3) the qualifiers and rebuttals (Tables 6.3, 6.4, and 6.5, respectively).

Categorizing fallacies in this manner—related to an insufficiency of information, issues with clarity of the reasoning, or to drawing a premature conclusion—provides a broader perspective from which to assess and

Table 6.3 Problems with Sufficiency/Quality of Evidence

Problems with Sufficiency/Quality of Evidence (Errors Regarding the Suitability of Proposed Grounds and Backing)

Argument from Incredulity	Rejecting novel claims or warrants on the basis they don't appear credible or conflict with prevailing thinking
Availability Bias	Restricting grounds or backing to the most easily accessed evidence, avoiding further study or examination
Confirmation Bias	Relying exclusively on grounds and backing that confirm a position while restricting counterarguments or evidence
Equivocation	Deliberately avoiding defining terms in warrants or claims or using terms in a manner different than would be most commonly understood
Hasty Generalization	Proposing a broad, unsubstantiated warrant, intending to deny need for or examination of other grounds or backing
Information Padding	Presenting an overwhelming volume of grounds and backing resulting in decreasing rather than increasing understanding
Reductionism	Attempting to dismiss complex issues or questions by offering short, simplistic responses that fail to provide adequate grounds or backing
Slippery Slope	Proposing that a series of negative cascading claims will result from an action or decision without providing necessary grounds or backing for the claim
Statistical Maneuvering	Presenting or withholding statistical grounds or backing in order to promote an incorrect or misleading interpretation of the information
Straw Man	Offering a weak or ridiculous parody of an opponent's argument that then can be mocked and totally dismissed without providing suitable backing

Table 6.4 Breaks in Reasoning

Breaks in Reasoning (Introduction of Irrelevant Grounds, Rebuttals, and Qualifiers)

A Priori Argument	Starting with the claim and then looking for backing
Ad Hominem	Refuting an argument by attacking the opposition
Appeal to Natural Law	Asserting that if something is "natural," it has to be good; conversely, things that are unnatural are bad
Appeal to Pity	Urging support for the underdog, irrespective of whether support is warranted
Appeal to Tradition	Assuming a conclusion, claim, or warrant is correct because that is the way things have always been or have always been done
Argument from Motives	Declaring an argument invalid owing to the questionable character or credibility of the individual making the claim

(Continued)

Table 6.4 (Continued)

Breaks in Reasoning (*Introduction of Irrelevant Grounds, Rebuttals, and Qualifiers*)

Circular Reasoning	Using the claim to prove itself: A causes B, therefore B causes A; or simply restating the claim differently as if introducing new grounds or backing
Cost Bias	Arguing that having paid a great cost to achieve something (money, effort, reputation), the thing being discussed must be valuable
False Analogy	Incorrectly comparing one thing to another in order to promote a false claim
Law of Unintended Consequences	Proclaiming *a priori* that sooner or later unforeseeable adverse side effects will occur consequent to a proposed claim
Non-Sequitur	Offering evidence, reasons, or conclusions that have no logical connection to the warrant or claim
Passive Voice Fallacy	Avoiding individual accountability or identification of sources by presenting information and positions using passive voice
Red Herring	Relying on an irrelevant argument or an unrelated but emotionally loaded issue in an attempt to distract from the main contention
Shifting the Burden of Proof	Challenging an opponent to disprove a claim rather than asking the person making the claim to defend his/her own argument
Tu Quoque	Excusing one's own bad action by pointing out that the opponent's acts, ideology, or character are as bad or worse than one's own
Worst-Case Fallacy	Promoting improbable, far-fetched, or imaginary worst-case scenarios rather than allow for realistic outcomes

Table 6.5 False or Rushed Conclusions

False or Rushed Conclusions (*Suggesting the Reliability of the Claim Requires/Allows No Further Analysis*)

Appeal to Closure	Asserting that a claim, no matter how questionable, must be accepted or the issue or argument will remain forever unsettled
Argument from Consequences	Arguing that something cannot be true because if it were, the consequences or outcome would be unacceptable or catastrophic
Argument from Ignorance	Arguing that because the needed evidence is either not known or not knowable, the claim must be accepted as presented (i.e., true or false)

(Continued)

Table 6.5 (Continued)

False or Rushed Conclusions (Suggesting the Reliability of the Claim Requires/Allows No Further Analysis)

Argument from Inertia	Proposing a claim be accepted solely because challenging it would constitute admission the idea/view/concept was wrong all along
Argumentum ex Silentio	Asserting an argument or claim must be accepted as presented (either true or false) because there is no evidence or proof to contradict it
Argumentum ad Populum	Arguing that because an opinion, view, or perspective is commonly shared or is voiced by someone senior, it must be accepted as correct
Complex Question	Requiring a simple answer (e.g., yes or no) to a question where qualifiers, rebuttals, and grounds demand a more nuanced response
False Dilemma	Offering only two possible options even though a broad range of possible alternatives, variations, and combinations are available

remedy the root cause of the shortcoming rather than expending effort to isolate and respond to each fallacy on a one-to-one basis.

Applying the Lessons

The types, volume, and focus of evidence provided to substantiate any persuasive argument—whether presented as a letter, email, report, or oral presentation—must reflect and integrate the lessons learned here and in each of the preceding chapters:

- Precisely discerning the scope, implications, and nuances of the subject;
- Determining the essential substantiation needed to invoke the intended response;
- Selecting language that most articulately and artfully communicates your thoughts;
- Facilitating comprehension of difficult and complex subject matter through purposeful visualization of information;
- Ensuring the presentation is tightly, exclusively, and immediately focused on the matter at hand; and
- Assessing the integrity and reliability of all components that comprise the argument.

Having learned and diligently applied these lessons in your communications, opportunities for advancement will arise, which leaves us with just one more set of techniques and strategies to consider. In Chapter 7 we will personalize the tools and lessons we have been examining by demonstrating how to take the fullest advantage of advancement opportunities by maximizing the messages communicated in your letter of application and resume and by employing a process that ensures the best possible performance during your job interview.

Notes

1 Anon, "The Greatest Villain in the History of Science," *The Renaissance Mathematicus*, December 19, 2015. https://thonyc.wordpress.com/2015/12/19/the-greatest-villain-in-the-history-of-science/#:~:text=In%20the%20popular%20version%20of,the%20front%20of%20Copernicus'%20De
2 Nicholas Copernicus, *On the Revolutions of Heavenly Spheres* (Amherst, New York: Prometheus Books, 1995).
3 Archimedes, "The Sand Reckoner," in *The Works of Archimedes*, ed. by T. L. Heath (Cambridge, England: Cambridge University Press, 1897), pp. 221–222.
4 Galileo, "A Sidereal Message," *Galileo: Selected Writings*, Translated: William R. Shea and Mark Davie (Oxford: Oxford University Press, 2012).
5 Octave Delepierre, *Historical Difficulties and Contested Events* (London, England: John Murray, 1868), p. 150.
6 Ibid.
7 Galileo, "Letter to Don Benedetto Castelli," in *Galileo: Selected Writings*.
8 Ibid.
9 Ibid.
10 Galileo, "Letter to the Grand Duchess Christina," in *Galileo: Selected Writings*.
11 Giorgio de Santillana, *The Crime of Galileo* (Chicago, IL: Chicago University Press, 1955).
12 John Paul II, "Address to the Plenary Session in Emergence of Complexity in Mathematics, Physics, Chemistry, and Biology," The Vatican, October 31, 1992. https://www.pas.va/en/magisterium/saint-john-paul-ii/1992-31-october.html#:~:text=Address%20to%20the%20Plenary%20Session,knowledge%20and%20to%20integrate%20learning'
13 Santillana, *Crimes of Galileo*.
14 John Dewey, *How We Think* (Memphis, TN: General Books, 2010).
15 Ibid.
16 Stephen Toulmin, Richard Rieke, Alan Janek, *An Introduction to Reasoning* (New York: McMillan Publishing, Co., 1979).
17 Stephen Toulmin, *Return to Reason* (Cambridge, MA: Harvard University Press, 2001).
18 Alan Monroe and Douglas Ehninger, *Principles of Speech Communication* (Glenview, IL: Scott, Foresman and Co., 1975).

Chapter 7

Applying Oneself

"The unpretentious, rather boring hall had been richly decorated … Just in front of the stage were three armchairs for royalty, and behind these was a semicircle of chairs for the prize winners, the presenters, and attendants. Back of the semicircle there were places for all the intellectuals, distinguished officials, and military officers from Stockholm and around the country. When the royal family was seated, the royal orchestra burst forth with a pompous festival overture by Ludwig Norman." And so, against this backdrop, as recounted by an eyewitness, on December 10, 1901—precisely five years to the date after the death of Alfred Nobel—the first five Nobel prizes were awarded at the Royal Swedish Academy of Music.[1]

Following in the footsteps of his father—who ran armaments factories and built underwater mines for Russia during the Crimean War, the first major successes among Alfred's 355 patents were the means to safely handle nitroglycerin accompanied by invention of the detonator and the blasting cap.

This new explosive, which he named "dynamite" for the Greek word *dynamis,* meaning "power," was subsequently supplanted by an even more powerful explosive and then, in 1887, with the patenting of ballistite, a smokeless nitroglycerin powder.

While traveling in France that following year, Alfred's brother, Ludvig, died from a heart attack. Believing it was Alfred who had passed away, one Paris newspaper published a scathing obituary announcing: "Le Marchand de la Mort est Mort" (the merchant of death is dead); The obituary then reads: "Dr. Alfred Nobel, who made a fortune by finding ways to kill more people faster than ever before, died yesterday."[2]

Having read the premature announcement of his death, Alfred supposedly became "obsessed with [his] posthumous reputation."[3] Far different from the obituary was his perception of how history should view his accomplishments: "My dynamite will sooner lead to peace than a thousand world [Geneva] conventions. As soon as men will find that in

DOI: 10.4324/9781003455585-8

one instant, whole armies can be utterly destroyed, they surely will abide by golden peace."[4]

In response to this "exaggerated" statement of his death (as Mark Twain remarked when encountering his own death notice in *The New York Sun*), in September 1895, unbeknownst to his heirs, Nobel revised his will bequeathing the majority of his fortune to "a cause upon which no future obituary writer would be able to cast aspersions."[5] More than 90% of his fortune (some $250 million) was to be set aside; the interest was, as stated in his will, to be "annually distributed in the form of prizes to those who, during the preceding year, shall have conferred the greatest benefit on mankind."[6]

But hurdles remained in reclaiming Alfred's legacy. Incensed at the terms of his will and the distribution of his vast fortune, some of Nobel's family members sought to have the will overturned. At the same time, Scandinavian institutions and government agencies argued the awards should concentrate exclusively on regional accomplishments. In addition, the various specifics regarding the selecting and awarding of prizes needed to be defined. Altogether, these factors resulted in a five-year hiatus between bequeathing the funding and holding the initial award ceremony.

Thereafter, over time, having been firmly established as, perhaps, the most prestigious award recognizing advances benefitting mankind, the Nobel Prize became the defining factor in Alfred Nobel's legacy and reputation, displacing the image of the "merchant of death," with recognition as one of the foremost patrons of progress.

Although our individual circumstances may not rival the celebrity of Nobel, the challenge of ensuring the proper recognition and acknowledgment of who we are—our merits, accomplishments, and potential contributions—occurs each time we pursue professional advancement. And, unlike Nobel who had both the resources and the time to recast his reputation and legacy, we, generally, are not afforded such allowances—or second chances.

Rather, pursuing new assignments is a practical test of abilities to apply the key lessons we have been considering:

- Making it easy for prospective employers to gage our preparedness,
- Being fully responsive to the position's expectations,
- Employing language that is artful and precise,
- Effectively displaying information,
- Responding crisply and succinctly,
- Presenting a convincing, "rational foundation" for selection.

The challenge, put simply, is whether we can skillfully, effectively, and persuasively articulate how our skills align with the company's mission;

whether our experience adds depth to the organization; and whether our personality is fitted to the corporate culture. Anything less is likely to be unsuccessful in securing the position.

Argument Not Inventory

"ALL men of whatsoever quality they be, who have done anything of excellence, or which may properly resemble excellence, ought, if they are persons of truth and honesty, to describe their life with their own hand."[7] So begins the 1562 *Autobiography of Benvenuto Cellini*, a celebrated Renaissance sculptor and goldsmith. This suggestion, from the earliest known autobiography, is a good starting point for generating our arguments for selection: Believing in oneself as the best candidate, offering a solid case for ourselves, and "describing" credentials with "truth and honesty."

Yet autobiographies, like Cellini's, are too broad, embedding detail in a broad intellectual history. At the other end of the spectrum, creating a simple historical catalog of what you've done is not enough. Nor is it sufficient to produce an application that looks exactly like all the others the company receives.

The challenge, rather, is to provide a consistent, discernable reasoning that alerts the company to points of differentiation from other candidates and announces the immediate applicability of credentials. It is a task that requires a disciplined methodology that creates the strongest possible case by

- isolating the most significant features of your career;
- precisely delineating your participation in accomplishments;
- giving initial shape to language—its precision, conciseness, and style;
- identifying personality traits (e.g., leadership) underpinning successes;
- establishing perspective on how your credentials should be perceived.

Done correctly, the methodology yields the basis for drafting the application letter, the design for structuring the resume, and the preparation for the job interview.

In the end, it is up to you—as we learned from the lesson of Nobel—whether to allow yourself to be defined by the hiring manager—someone who may not recognize the full import of your credentials, or, instead, to use your application package to argue conclusively for your selection.

Arguing Your Case

The design and contents of your resume, the crafting of your letter of application, and your ability to articulate your particular strengths during

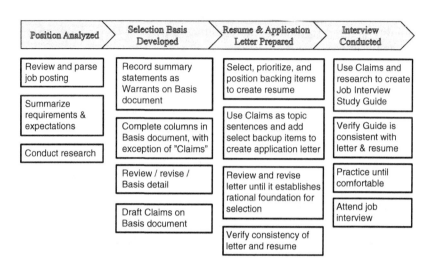

Figure 7.1 Shaping the Argument for Selection.

the job interview must all be presented as a consistent argument for selection. It is a process, as depicted in Figure 7.1, that consists of 4 segments comprised of 15 steps.

Position Analyzed

Rather than conducting an inventory of experience, building an argument, as we have learned, begins by establishing a precise knowledge of points that need to be argued. It is a process, as defined by Dewey, Toulmin, and Monroe, that begins with defining the "difficulty," which, in our case, means delineating the exact dimensions of the hiring company's needs.

Accordingly, the exercise begins by dissecting the job posting. However, because it is unreasonable to expect a one-to-one correspondence between qualifications cited in the posting and one's credentials, the transcription of the posting's expectations is then converted into statements summarizing the qualifications needed. These summary statements allow for a broadened perception of how to align credentials and make more visible the lines of argument that will produce a persuasive response. (Table 7.1 illustrates these first two steps using a job posting for a Senior Facility Manager.)

Table 7.1 Job Posting and Summarization

Senior Facility Manager—Hydrogen Generation Facility Portland, Oregon

Detail Transcribed from Published Posting	*Summarization of Requirements*
Qualifications	*Experience*
• BA/BS in Engineering, Management, or related field, • Minimum fifteen years' experience in a technical, operations, or engineering organization, • Demonstrated career progression of increased responsibilities, • Ability to obtain national certification in quality control, • Demonstrated ability to write, edit, and review technical documents, • Advanced skills with standard office products, • Chemical manufacturing experience and previous experience with Federal regulators or chemical licensing agencies are desirable.	• General management of complex technical facilities and large diverse organizations • Familiarity with new chemical processing technology • Experience in all phases of facility operation • Proficiency in project management systems • Productive relations with unions and external entities
Responsibilities	*Management style*
• Provide commissioning and management of a state-of-the-art hydrogen generation facility. • Manage operations, engineering, safety, and maintenance. • Ensure safe and compliant performance of all facility operations. • Maintain facility schedules, resource allocations, and production commitments. • Align activities with interfacing organizations. • Promote continuous improvement in performance and safety. • Provide for the appropriate training and development of personnel. • Maintain communication and coordination with experts, peers, senior management, union leadership, regulators, and stakeholders. • Practice the highest standards of ethical business conduct. • Demonstrate commitment to the corporate values.	• Strong ethics • Team orientation • Open communications

That response, to be successful, must present credentials that demonstrate six factors:

1 a reasonable knowledge of the company, its goals and mission,
2 an understanding of relevant company challenges and opportunities,
3 a purposely organized presentation of applicable credentials and capabilities,
4 a clearly delineated image of potential and anticipated contributions,
5 a substantive degree of equivalency between past accomplishments and projected successes, and
6 a reasoned forecasting of the significance and magnitude of anticipated contributions.

In accomplishing these goals, it must be recognized that job postings infrequently provide significant insight into the company's character, mission, and strategic directions. Gaining perspective on what has prompted the posting of the position (e.g., expansion, loss of talent) as well as details on short- and long-term corporate challenges and opportunities need to be discovered through research that considers information issued by the company (e.g., annual reports) and in industry publications.

Continuing with our posting for a Senior Facility Manager, let's assume research has identified the following information immediately pertinent to the position:

• In the last year, the company lost a major client owing to missed production commitments resulting from downtime of critical equipment and delays in subcontracted work.
• The company's primary product is hydrogen for use in heating, but the company has signaled a shift to producing aviation fuel, a faster-growing and more sustainable market.
• Twice in the last three years, the Environmental Protection Agency (EPA) has cited the facility for higher than acceptable hydrogen concentrations in the plant.
• The plant relies on an early production technology that is more complicated and less adaptable to scaling up than other production methods.

Selection Basis Developed

Using details from the job posting coupled with insights from the research, the candidate can—using Toulmin's language and his anatomy of argument—capture the components of an argument for selection in a format that will provide for ready translation into the letter of application, the resume, and preparation for use in the job interview. This format (Table 7.2)—a "Basis of Argument for Selection" (Basis) form—consists

Table 7.2 Recording the Argument for Selection

Warrant	Grounds/Backing	Qualifiers	Rebuttal	Significance	CLAIM
1 Managed complex technical facilities/large organizations	• Managed high-hazard facilities • Obtained hazardous operations certification • Instituted standards-based management	No hydrogen-related experience	Experience with similar hazardous chemicals/rare gases	Related experience allows quickly coming up-to-speed	My recent assignments provide directly applicable experience (scope and responsibility)
2 Familiarity with new chemical processing technology	• Oversaw design and procurement of new/advanced technologies • Developed technology assessment program	Do not have requested certification. Reduced accidents by 35%	Provided significant input. Certification obtainable	Can infuse transferrable knowledge/adding valuable perspective	My experience with new technologies and optimization will be beneficial in charting modernization effort
3 Experience in all phases of facility operation	• Led startup testing, commissioning on major facility redesign • Closed out major project	Boosted production by 72% through process redesign	—	Unique breadth of management experience.	I have had first-hand leadership roles in all project phases, from initiation to closeout

(Continued)

Table 7.2 (Continued)

Warrant	Grounds/Backing	Qualifiers	Rebuttal	Significance	CLAIM
4 Proficiency in earned value management	• Managed schedules, costs, risk management • Developed multi-year system operating plan • Earned Value Management System (EVMS) certified	—	—	Significant EVMS expertise	In addition to being EVMS certified, I managed the project control organization
5 Productive relations: un-ions/regulators	• Negotiated union contracts • Provided liaison with regulators	—	—	Proven record of cooperation	I have a history of successful relationships with unions and regulators
6 Ethical per-formance	• Won manager of the year two years in a row	Not certain how to demonstrate!	No infractions(?)	Excellent evaluations (?)	Practicing and demanding high ethical standards

Research Identified Company Issues/Opportunities for Tailoring Credentials

Issue/Opportunity	Credential to Emphasize	Benefit to Company	Alignment
Company recently missed major deadlines	Record of 98+% on-time commitment delivery	Enhancement of performance management system	Warrants 2 & 4
Company received EPA safety citings	Developed award-winning safety controls	Introduction of proven practices for improving industrial safety	Warrants 1 & 2
Plant is an aging facility/new technology needed	• Optimization experience • Led facility redesign	Application of proven processes for disciplined facility upgrades	Warrants 2, 3, & 4

Warrant Summary statement of specified qualifications/expectations of position being sought.
Grounds/Backing: Principal and secondary substantiation of qualification.
Qualifiers: Explanation of strengths or weaknesses of grounds and backing.
Rebuttals: Explanation of any compensating factors for weaknesses or qualifications not met.
Significance: Proposed benefits to company.
Claim: Thematic statement encapsulating qualification relative to the warrant.

of six columns that collectively comprise the "rational foundation" for securing the position:

> *Warrants*: The statements summarizing the qualifications cited in the posting
> *Grounds/Backing*: Principal and secondary substantiation demonstrating how qualifications are met (or exceeded)
> *Qualifiers*: Conditions (e.g., challenges, unique circumstances) that clarify, add specificity, or define relevance of the grounds or backing
> *Rebuttals*: Compensating factors that respond to perceived gaps or weaknesses in the grounds/backing (e.g., equivalencies)
> *Significance*: Anticipated benefits to the company from your selection (e.g., enhanced company leadership)
> *Claims*: Statements encapsulating the message communicated in the preceding five columns.

Further, the main points identified in the research are summarized in the final rows of the form.

Building the Application Package

With the Basis form completed, all three components of the application package—the letter of application, resume, and the preparation for the job interview—can be prepared. Importantly, that preparation can now ensure the argument is not only fully responsive to the posting, but also that the three pieces will complement one another in communicating a powerful and consistent message:

- The letter of application will lay out the themes of the argument.
- The resume will detail the substance of the qualifications.
- The job interview will establish alignment between credentials and company's needs.

As such, the application package goes well beyond an inventory, representing an integrated and disciplined sales or marketing exercise: The letter of application represents getting your foot in the door; the resume makes the pitch; and the job interview is the handclasp that closes the deal.

Alternatively described using Monroe's sequencing of argument (Chapter 6), collectively the three pieces present the argument consistent with "the thought-line that most people are accustomed to following":

- The letter of application concentrates on fulfilling the attention and need steps—laying out the "claims" for selection;

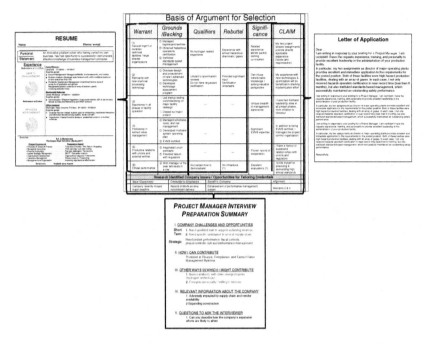

Figure 7.2 The Foundations of the Application Package.

- The resume fulfills the satisfaction step—offering specifics that speak to the expectations from both the job posting and research; and
- The interview completes the visualization and action steps—distinguishing the unique capacity to address the company's "difficulties."

As depicted in Figure 7.2, the Basis form just completed underpins development of all three pieces of the application package. The column on Claims forms the principal substance of the Letter of application. The warrants and the grounds provide the details of the resume. And a synthesized and abbreviated combination of the research and claims produces the job interview study guide.

The Letter of Application

Not all job postings, especially when pursuing advances within the same corporation, require a letter of application. But, even in those instances, drafting a letter is still the most effective means of honing themes that will run throughout the application process.

Table 7.3 Translating Claims into the Application Letter

Claims	Opening Paragraphs of the Application Letter
My two project director assignments provide directly applicable experience (scope and responsibility)—Claim 1	I am writing in response to your posting for a Senior Facility Manager. I am confident I have the requisite experience, training, and professionalism to provide excellent leadership in the administration of your production facility.
My experience with new technologies and optimization will be beneficial in charting modernization efforts—Claim 2	In particular, my current assignment at HTG as Facility Manager—following assignments as senior systems engineer, engineering manager, and chief facility engineer—provides experience directly applicable to your position.
I have had first-hand leadership roles in all project phases, from initiation to closeout—Claim 3	At four different high-hazard facilities producing an array of rare gases, my leadership contributed to a 35% reduction in industrial safety concerns while achieving a 72% improvement in process efficiency through the introduction of new technologies.

Whereas in the Basis form claims are recorded on a warrant-by-warrant basis to allow for thorough assessment of their strengths, for use in the application letter, several claims might be synthesized into a single statement, rephrased, or reprioritized—however best reinforces the argument. For example, Table 7.3 illustrates how the first three claims on the Basis form translate into the opening paragraphs of the application letter.

Once these thematic statements—the application's topic sentences—have been polished to the point they precisely, thoroughly, and concisely relate to the argument, do you move on to preparation of the resume.

The Resume

Within the limitations of the process established by the hiring company for the submittal of applications (e.g., pdf, online forms), it is not the individual pieces of information but rather their role in advancing the argument that defines the character of the resume.

It is not true that all resumes must look alike, must contain precisely the same headings, or must present information in precisely the same sequence. That strategy of blending in with all the other resumes is the exact opposite of what is needed: Each resume, each application, must be individually designed with the intent of meeting the qualifications while, at the same time, artfully and persuasively differentiating oneself from the

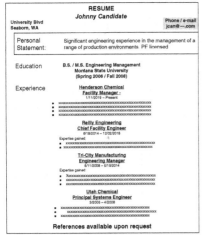
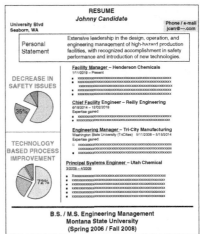

Figure 7.3 A Comparison of Resume Effectiveness.

competition. Accomplishing these goals requires a resume whose visual impact amplifies the message and advances the argument.

Rather than relying on rigid templates or fixed conceptions of a professional resume, design factors such as the resume's substance, length, and organization need to be governed by the same two criteria we applied when we examined the visualization of information practiced by Minard, Snow and Nightingale: Effectiveness in Communicating Purpose and Effectiveness in the Visualization of Information.

As example of varying design features to strengthen an argument for selection, Figure 7.3 depicts two versions of the resume of our candidate for Senior Facility Manager. The resume on the left adheres to the standard guidance. The resume on the right reflects tailoring of the design and sequencing of information to emphasize points of differentiation (differences summarized in Table 7.4 using criteria adapted from the visualization of information scorecard used in Chapter 4).

Interview Preparation and Delivery

Perhaps the area of the application process least addressed in the literature is the process of preparing for the job interview. Rather than providing for a disciplined process, standard guidance suggests candidates review their resumes and rehearse answers to commonly asked questions. This guidance implicitly assumes there is no reasonable means of taking

Table 7.4 A Comparative Analysis

Resume Assessment

Communicating Purpose			Visualization of Information		
ATTRIBUTE	Standard Format	Tailored Format	**ATTRIBUTE**	Standard Format	Tailored Format
INFORMATION SUFFICIENT	Information responsive to job posting	Additional grounds and backing capture results of research	**LAYOUT ATTRACTIVE**	Standard	Font, type sizes, vertical separations enhance visualization of argument
INFORMATION CLEAR	Statements taken directly from Basis form	Information targeted; graphics added to amplify narrative	**POINTS OF DIFFERENTIATION EVIDENT**	No specifics identified	Graphics added to highlight areas of keen company interest
INFORMATION EFFECTIVELY ORGANIZED	Standard organization used	Experience placed before education; job titles given precedence	**STRUCTURE FREE FROM DISTRACTIONS**	No points of evident emphasis	Bolded text; graphics; and repositioning of experience ensure focus of attention
INFORMATION CONVINCING	All qualifications met	Personal statement rewritten based on claims; detail expanded	**STRUCTURE REINFORCES MESSAGE**	Qualification established	Presentation emphasizes lines of argument and items of differentiation
SUMMARY EVALUATION					
QUALIFICATION DEMONSTRATED	Acceptable	Qualifications amplified by backing, design, and research	**PERSUASIVE VISUALIZATION**	Standard presentation	Format, graphics, typefaces, and sequencing visually reinforce message

control of the interview, no strategy to ensure you're able to make a convincing case for selection. However, that conclusion is wrong.

The breadth of information captured on the Basis form likely exceeds the amount that can be reasonably retained and recalled, particularly during the stress of an interview. That is why an Interview Preparation Summary guide, a manageable and retainable synopsis, is needed.

Emphasizing the proposed argument, level of detail in the guide maximizes its utility: Abbreviated statements of the corporate challenges and opportunities are first complemented by potential contributions the candidate offers the company. Then critical research is summarized, followed by questions to put to the interviewer. To further aid in retention and recall, information is displayed using distinctive headings, segregated by large areas of white space, and captured in short, simple sentences (Table 7.5).

This level of detail and design also provides flexibility in how to use the information. This flexibility is key to providing responses that are not only

Table 7.5 Sample Interview Preparation Guide

Senior Facility Manager **Interview Preparation Summary**	
I *Company Challenges and Opportunities*	
Short Term	1 Needs experience in high-hazard, chemical production facilities 2 Needs project management and safety management leadership
Strategic	1 Transitioning to new hydrogen production 2 Coordination of facility upgrades/equipment replacement technology
II HOW CAN I CONTRIBUTE?	
	1 Experience in facility redesign/introduction of new technology 2 EVMS certification and extensive project management expertise 3 Defined and implemented safety control programs 4 Experience in all phases of facility design and operation
III OTHER WAYS IN WHICH I MIGHT CONTRIBUTE	
	1 Translatable experience managing other hazardous gases 2 Senior management representative on union contract negotiations 3 Developed new technology assessment program 4 GSA (General Services Administration) training in contractor management

(Continued)

Table 7.5 (Continued)

Senior Facility Manager Interview Preparation Summary
IV *RELEVANT INFORMATION ABOUT THE COMPANY*
1 Citations from EPA for issues with industrial safety 2 Aging facility requiring upgrades or redesign 3 Improvements needed in subcontractor management
V *QUESTIONS TO ASK THE INTERVIEWER*
1 Do you plan on upgrading the facility to new technology? 2 How do you envision the future hydrogen market? 3 What do you consider will be my primary focus—initially/long term?

thorough, but also fitted to the flow of the conversation—something that cannot be achieved with rehearsed answers. For example, below are three different responses the candidate might use depending on the flow of the conversation to answer the question "Why the interest in the position?":

- Beginning with a reference to the research and then highlighting relevant credentials:
  "I am excited about using my experience in process enhancement and technology assessment in helping to shape the facility's redesign."
- Beginning by citing a particular capability and then expanding on its applicability:
  "In addition to my experience with facility management, I am hoping to apply my certification in Earned Value Management Systems to working with support staff and subcontractors."
- Beginning by highlighting professional attributes to show alignment with the corporate culture:
  "Coming from an organization that did not always work effectively with the regulators, I look forward to helping enhancing teamwork with unions, stakeholders, and regulators."

A Concluding Note

As noted in the book's Introduction, to achieve a level of skill for which one is recognized as an accomplished communicator in contemporary business and industry is contingent on being prepared to deal effectively with the complexity, urgency, and significance of assignments that routinely arise in management and corporate leadership.

Throughout this text, you have been learning the lessons that provide that capability, lessons that now equip you to deliver communications that will distinguish you as a promotable individual, a professional ready and prepared to assume increased levels of responsibility.

By putting the lessons learned into play in your day-to-day assignments, you can demonstrate to colleagues and your management that you command the *"Strategies that Advance Careers"* and are fully capable of applying the *"Art of Professional Communication."*

Notes

1   Folke Henschen, "From the First Nobel Prize Award Ceremony, 1901," December 10, 1975, https://www.nobelprize.org/ceremonies/from-the-first-nobel-prize-award-ceremony-1901.
2   Van Andrews, "Did a Premature Obituary Inspire the Nobel Prize?" *History*, July 23, 2020, https://www.history.com/news/did-a-premature-obituary-inspire-the-nobel-prize.
3   Andrews, "Did a Premature Obituary Inspire the Nobel Prize?"
4   Troy Lennon, "Swedish Inventor Alfred Nobel Was Spurred by His Obituary to Create the Nobel Prize," *The Daily Telegraph*, December 13, 2023, https://www.dailytelegraph.com.au/news/swedish-inventor-alfred-nobel-was-spurred-by-his-obituary-to-create-the-nobel-prize/news-story/c134de38fb4f3ebefef06b2 11b0527d5.
5   Andrews, "Did a Premature Obituary Inspire the Nobel Prize?"
6   Andrews, "Did a Premature Obituary Inspire the Nobel Prize?"
7   Benvenuto Cellini, *The Autobiography of Benvenuto Cellini*, trans. Anne McDonnell (New York: Alfred A. Knopf, 2010).

Index

Note: page numbers in **bold** refer to "tables" and *italicized* locators denote "figures"

Printed in the United States
by Baker & Taylor Publisher Services